HELPING
YOUNG CHILDREN AT
RISK

HELPING YOUNG CHILDREN AT RISK

---/---

A Psycho-Educational Approach

Agnes M. Plenk

Foreword by
RUDOLF EKSTEIN

Westport, Connecticut
London

Library of Congress Cataloging-in-Publication Data

Plenk, Agnes M.
    Helping young children at risk : a psycho-educational approach /
Agnes M. Plenk ; foreword by Rudolf Ekstein.
        p.   cm.
    Includes bibliographical references and index.
    ISBN 0-275-94591-X (alk. paper).—ISBN 0-275-94592-8 (pbk. :
alk. paper)
    1. Psychiatric day treatment for children. 2. Group psychotherapy
for children. 3. Behavior disorders in children—Treatment.
4. Children's Center (Salt Lake City, Utah) I. Title.
RJ504.53.P54   1993
618.92′89152—dc20   93-20303

British Library Cataloguing in Publication Data is available.

Library of Congress Catalog Card Number: 92-20303
ISBN: 0-275-94591-X
        0-275-94592-8 (pb)

First published in 1993

Praeger Publishers, 88 Post Road West, Westport, CT 06881
An imprint of Greenwood Publishing Group, Inc.

Printed in the United States of America

The paper used in this book complies with the
Permanent Paper Standard issued by the National
Information Standards Organization (Z39.48–1984).

10 9 8 7 6 5 4 3 2 1

Contents

following the development of the model from a distance. It is enjoyable to see the bridge created between psychoanalysis, clinical psychology, and education, all used in the best interest of at risk children. In different ways we have endeavored to create islands of safety and understanding leading to emotional health for children, help for parents to be better parents, and directly and indirectly improve our school settings.

There is no doubt that preventive programs at a young age are cost effective in dollars and in human values. We do not have to wait until children with serious disabilities fail in public school and fall behind. The work done at The Children Center is also a practical example of successful community participation in a pioneering venture. I can only wish that this volume will find many readers, will stimulate new ways of working with emotionally disturbed young children and their families and also in the training of those who have a heart for children.

My hope is that the message contained in the pages of this book will reach many people as it travels around the country and I am happy that my few words can accompany it on its voyage.

Rudolf Ekstein

Foreword

I have known the author, Agnes Mero Plenk, for a good many years. We both became interested working with children in Vienna, discovering psychoanalytic pedagogy, influenced by Freudian and Adlerian thinking. We met again in America, I working at the Menninger Foundation and Dr. Plenk as research assistant to Dr. Franz Alexander, Director of the Chicago Psychoanalytic Institute.

Dr. Plenk's work with children goes back to 1946 and has continued through the years. Working in academic medicine as Senior psychologist in the Department of Psychiatry at the University of Utah and in private practice convinced her of the great need for a community agency for young children with behavior problems.

She founded The Children's Center in Salt Lake City in 1963 and remained its energetic and charismatic leader until 1986, focusing on treating young, emotionally disturbed children and teaching graduate students in the mental health and education fields.

The treatment techniques developed at the Children's Center and refined over the years could well be applied in other communities and in other settings. The continuum of mental health services for young children, including educational, community, and therapeutic aspects within an affordable framework are long overdue. It is hoped that this book with its detailed information on assessment techniques, eclectic intervention methods and approaches to creative activities will motivate mental health professionals and teachers to action. Stress on an interdisciplinary team using a developmental and psychodynamic approach combined with chapters on administration provides rich material for further experimentation.

I have maintained contact with Dr. Plenk through all these years and have often had the privilege of participating in the program as well as

Preface

Very few people are fortunate enough to leave behind them a legacy that is not a technological invention, a means to make war more effective, or something that brings economic rewards to a few. In a society where children come last rather than first, where ruined lives are patched up instead of problems being prevented, a legacy that creates a small island of hope and change is indeed a rarity.

I am among the fortunate ones who have been able to translate a dream into reality. This book shares some of the ideas and practices that have been an outgrowth of that dream. Pronouncements about family values and the preciousness of childhood are a meaningless sham unless the damaging conditions in which many children live are acknowledged and practical steps are taken to improve the lives of these children.

An example of such an undertaking is The Children's Center in Salt Lake City, in many ways an unlikely place for social experimentation because of the essentially conservative nature of the community. In the 1950s and 1960s Salt Lake City experienced a great influx of young professional people wanting preschool services for their children. To meet this need, the Center originated as a regular preschool in a new community church. After a short while, physically, intellectually, and emotionally handicapped children were admitted. By 1963 the specialized needs of children with behavioral problems necessitated a move into a separate building. With the help of the community, a private nonprofit, nonsectarian agency was formed. Under my leadership and that of a psychiatrist, The Children's Center has grown over the years to two day-treatment centers serving seventy children each and a group home for nine children.

This book is an outgrowth of the clinical, administrative, and advocacy experience that I gained during the growth and development of the Center. Much of it has been locally disseminated in speeches to professional and parent groups, during a radio call-in program, in articles in local publications, and to students on the university level. Nationally, some of the students trained at the Center have used the day-treatment group therapy model in mental health centers, in schools, and with some modifications in private practice.

Therapy for young children with emotional problems is a greatly neglected field despite the fact that much lip service is given to early intervention. An activity group therapy model provides the opportunity to change behavior patterns in a theoretically sound and affordable way. My experience in the late 1940s as a psychologist in a large midwestern inner-city psychiatric agency and the growth and success of The Children's Center are proof that the model is highly effective in changing the behavior of children.

In 1986 I retired from the position of executive director, but I have remained on the staff as supervisor of pre- and postdoctoral students in psychology. In recent years, under medically trained leadership, a mother-toddler program and training for medical residents have been added.

A community agency built on a shoestring budget can maintain itself only with the help of untold devoted and committed parents and professionals. They have unstintingly supported me and, with their help, we have built a unique and model facility. In addition, financial support provided by the State Division of Human Services, Mental Health, and the United Way of Salt Lake City, and by many individuals and local and national foundations has been a source of personal satisfaction. Without their help, The Children's Center might have remained only a dream.

ACKNOWLEDGMENTS

I would like to express my appreciation to the staff of The Children's Center; in particular, to Dr. Douglas Goldsmith, who patiently and constructively offered valuable suggestions. The editorial assistance of Dr. Helen Hodgson and the clerical expertise of Helen Eckersley helped me through many pitfalls. This book could not have been written without the help, understanding, and good humor of my husband, Dr. Henry Plenk.

All names and dates in the cases reported have been changed to maintain confidentiality.

Introduction

As a treatment modality, activity group therapy has been frequently mislabeled, misunderstood, and relegated to the back burner of therapeutic techniques. It has been used as an umbrella term for many modalities that have only one thing in common, namely, that two or more clients are seen by a therapist in a therapeutic encounter. However, many other variables, such as theoretical background, length of treatment, group composition, role of the therapist, and purpose of the group, can be used to distinguish these modalities.

The oldest and most traditional form of group therapy with children was based on Slavson's pioneering work (1943), which had a definite psychoanalytical orientation. His method excluded aggressive, seriously withdrawn, and psychotic children, thus limiting its usefulness to a relatively small group of children. It also excluded children under the age of five.

The character of behavioral problems has changed greatly since Slavson's efforts. Theories have advanced, society has changed, and the problems of the children he excluded have become of paramount importance. Aggressive, predelinquent children need early and intensive intervention if later, more severe problems for them and for society are to be avoided. Building more correctional facilities for the young is no answer to the problems of gangs and to the increasingly severe crimes being committed by adolescents.

The activity group therapy model developed at The Children's Center has taken Slavson's group therapy model and made it useful for the present generation of children. Fantasies of using psychoanalytic techniques to save the world have not proven effective, though they are extremely helpful to a small number of individuals. In contrast, the model employed by The Children's Center is based on intensive early intervention with children between the ages of two and five. Daily three-hour group sessions for children and counseling for the parents are offered.

This book is not a theoretical treatise but an outgrowth of the experiences gained during the thirty-year existence of The Children's Center. The methods of intervention used to help children develop trust, recognize limits, express feelings in a socially acceptable way, and learn alternative behaviors combine behavioral, cognitive, and psychodynamic techniques. Practical applications of these techniques are described in the different chapters and supported with examples and case histories. The members of the interdisciplinary treatment team, including less frequently used but important members such as movement and speech professionals, are identified in conjunction with a description of the roles they fulfill on the team. Activities are outlined that draw on the strengths of the child rather than on pathological and diagnostic categories.

The book stresses individual temperamental differences, rather than group stereotypes. It also views preconceived theoretical ideas as subordinate concepts in the development of a treatment plan to meet the needs of a specific child.

Having served the Salt Lake Valley for thirty years, The Children's Center is a model in the use of activity group therapy with young children exhibiting a diversity of disabilities. This treatment modality has been field tested in day-care centers, preschools, public school classrooms, and family day-care settings. With statistics indicating that between 5 percent and 10 percent of children show behavioral or learning disabilities, affordable preventive measures are urgently needed. Communities have to develop intervention modalities to serve these larger numbers of children in a more economical way. The intent of this book is to give other professionals and communities the impetus to develop programs similar to that which has proven so successful at The Children's Center.

Chapter 1
Theoretical Framework

INTRODUCTION

The recently implemented federal legislation has renewed and increased interest in intervention programs for children at risk who have a variety of disabilities. In most states, federal funding for these programs is channeled through the school districts, which, in many instances, are already overwhelmed with a multitude of problems. Large classes, multiethnic groups, and limited funding have made the teaching of academics truly a challenge.

To add special-needs children to this load demands special techniques; in the best of all worlds, these children would participate in preventive programs before entering the public school system. Preventive programs are potentially much more cost-effective both in dollars and cents and in human values than waiting until children with disabilities enter public school. Children who are preoccupied with unresolved negative feelings of failure in interpersonal relationships, traumas, and a low self-concept have difficulty using their cognitive abilities. When compared to latency-age youngsters or adolescents, preschool children are more pliable and more apt to make changes within a favorable environment.

Historically, traditional medical models as practiced in child guidance clinics did not adequately serve many seriously disturbed children; and therapists in private offices excluded children who lived in poverty, resulting in large numbers of unserved, emotionally troubled children. For the past thirty years The Children's Center in Salt Lake City has pioneered an intensive, community-based activity group therapy model for the treatment of young, emotionally disturbed children. Over the years we have witnessed a steady increase in referrals, now risen to alarming proportions. At this time the Center averages ten to fifteen referrals in weekly intake meetings. A major change and even more alarming trend can be seen in the type and seriousness of disorders.

CHANGES IN THE NATURE OF REFERRALS

Children used to be referred by pediatricians for problems of bodily functions such as eating, sleeping, or bowel and bladder control. Then followed a period of increased concern with regard to limited or total lack of speech. Withholding of speech, at times leading to elective mutism, was recognized as a serious problem. Although children with these problems are still referred, they have assumed secondary importance to children referred for disturbances of affect and social behaviors. Problems with expression of affect range from prolonged crying spells to fearfulness, anxiety, overdependency, separation anxiety, and depression on the one hand, the so-called internalizers, to serious antisocial manifestations of acting-out behaviors on the other, the externalizers. A continuum of problems of noncompliance, threats of bodily harm toward siblings and peers, fire setting, and cruelty to animals is not unusual any more in preschool children. Hyperactivity and attention deficit disorders range high on the list of referrals, but frequently they are only manifestations of depression or anxiety.

The most serious change is the increasing number of referrals for sexual and physical abuse. The children referred with these concerns fall in the extreme categories of aggression or withdrawal and uniformly suffer from extremely damaged self-esteem. In the event of sexual abuse, the telltale signs are sexual precocity, excessive masturbation, and seductive behaviors toward adults and peers. These experiences have been so traumatic that social skills were never learned or have been totally lost.

Though some of these changes are undoubtedly due to more specific methods of diagnosis and to progress in research on the biological origins of psychological disturbances, consideration must also be given to the tremendous societal changes that have occurred and, unfortunately, their negative influence on many families. These changes necessitate innovative approaches. Professionals in different behavioral disciplines need to examine ways to provide help for the growing number of emotionally disturbed children. The model developed at The Children's Center is one such effort (Plenk, 1978).

WHY GROUP INTERVENTION?

A therapeutic group setting provides a natural arena in which to develop social skills for traumatized children. Early intervention is essential, as most children will spend the largest part of their lives for the next twelve years with age mates trying to master cognitive tasks. A positive self-image, skills in conflict resolution, and confidence in forming relationships are essential prerequisites for functioning adequately in an academic setting.

Many young children who have had unhappy experiences with "big people" will feel more comfortable solving problems in a group with peers than in a one-to-one situation with a strange adult. Two- and three-year-olds are beginning to look at peers with interest, wondering about little persons similar but different from themselves. The conflicts that the children bring with them will spontaneously replay in a peer group, and their solutions will be the basis for behavioral changes.

THE CHILDREN

Presently available diagnostic labels for young children with emotional problems, needed mostly for billing purposes, are only minimally useful for treatment planning or grouping. This is particularly true for two-year-olds, who often are referred for lack of speech, abuse and neglect, hyperactivity, dependency, and lack of interest in gaining autonomy.

Three-year-olds' referral symptoms are similar, except that many of these children show definite symptoms of depression, such as sleeping and eating problems, and self-destructive behaviors. It seems that they have given up getting the attention and care they need.

Michael, 3 years, 6 months of age, was referred by his day-care center for withdrawal from his peers, prolonged crying spells, and mood swings. Some days he would cling to the adult caretaker; on others he refused to be picked up. He totally lacked trust in his environment.

Another frequent reason for the referral of a three-year-old is the child's use of excessive tantrums to gain immediate gratification.

Aggressive children who have had earlier traumatic experiences as results of acting-out behaviors such as rejection, withdrawal of love, physical and verbal punishment—yes, even abuse—will need to experience the matter-of-fact handling of such incidents by the therapists in charge. By seeing alternative behaviors modeled by children and adults, aggressive children can learn new ways of handling angry feelings without the feared consequences. Children learn from each other under the guidance of trained therapists. It is reassuring to be in the presence of adults who solve conflicts, suggest new behaviors, and patiently and skillfully maintain an atmosphere of acceptance.

GROUPING

In the treatment of young children, daily groups provide a stable environment. Weekly or alternate-day sessions mean new adjustments to the children in the group and renewed separation from the parents. As separation anxiety is a frequent problem of emotionally disturbed preschool children, care must be taken to minimize opportunities for its occurrence in a therapeutic setting.

Each group consists of a maximum of eight to nine children, functionally, behaviorally, and chronologically matched within six months. Size and composition of the group have proven to be most important. For positive group dynamics, a tolerable noise level, and optimal observation, nine children are a maximum. We prefer to place only eight children in our group of two-year-olds, as these children are frequently our most emotionally deprived and need much physical outreach. Groups smaller than eight or nine do not appear to be helpful because therapy seems to revert to individual therapy in a group setting rather than therapy through the group process. Some children become anxious and regress when the groups are too small because they consequently receive too much individual attention. On the other hand, other children make great strides when the group is smaller, as, for example, during an epidemic of chicken pox; we take this as a sign that individual therapy sessions, in addition to the group sessions, might be beneficial.

Heterogenous grouping of children is essential for productive interaction in this treatment model. In our experience, a group of nine acting-out, oppositional children does not help the treatment process but reinforces the pathological patterns that prevail when no peer modeling of acceptable behavior is available. A homogenous group of withdrawn children might prove equally taxing, reinforcing their type of negative behavior and stressing the emotional reserves of staff.

Placement of children who have good or at least adequate language skills with children who have poor or no speech is another important consideration. For children who do not function age-appropriately in one or more areas, chronological placement in a group is of secondary importance. Consider the following case.

Susie was a preemie, born with a severe hearing problem, and at 3 years, 6 months of age was not yet toilet trained, was overly active, and engaged in severe power struggles with adults. She was the only girl and youngest child in a family of four. Evaluation showed that Susie was functioning on a superior level in all nonverbal areas. She was placed in a group of children all at least twelve months younger and including three other girls.

Placement in a younger group permitted Susie to function generally on a lower level and to excel in small-motor and cognitive areas. Being looked up to by the other children because of these accomplishments helped Susie gain self-confidence and eliminated pressure. Lack of toilet training was not much of an issue with the other children, and within the framework of general acceptance, Susie very quickly gained bladder and bowel control. Power struggles decreased, and her lowered anxiety level also lowered her activity level. A month prior to discharge, she was moved into an age-appropriate group to try out her newly learned skills on her peers. She functioned well and maintained progress.

A mixture of acting-out and withdrawn children, mute and verbal children, boys and girls, seems to offer the best environment for emotional growth, ego development, and the learning of alternative behaviors. Limiting the groups to only one type of disturbance deprives the children of one of the most effective agents of change: peer modeling.

The anxious child sees acceptance of negative affect without anger and retaliation by the adult and thereby gains confidence in expressing feelings. This realization will give them courage to break their pattern of withdrawal and experiment with healthier behaviors. The acting-out child realizes security because attacks on other children or adults and destruction of property are not sanctioned. The "total permissiveness" paradigm is not accepted, for experience has shown that many children with poor ego structure will judge permissiveness as weakness and continue to push for limits.

The withholding, frequently angry child will learn that expression of negative feelings is acceptable and in time will acquire emotional freedom.

Katy, 3 years, 6 months of age, was referred by her pediatrician for lack of ability to relate to children and selective mutism with strangers and even some family members. She had been sent to a nursery school in the hope that wishing to interact with children would help her. After Katy remained mute for three months at nursery school, she was referred to The Children's Center.

Katy was a large, somber-looking, middle child of a professional couple. Her minimal communication paid off at home because she gained attention, particularly from her father, a rather remote, nonverbal person himself. His example reinforced her distancing behavior and made changes outside the family circle even more difficult.

Rather than pressing Katy to speak, adults accepted her mutism and peers acknowledged it. She was provided with all sorts of expressive materials like water, paints, and clay. At first she attacked all materials aggressively and refused to take any paintings home. Social interaction improved on a nonverbal level, consisting for some time of pushing a small car to a child who also had a considerable speech delay. Katy began to talk on the playground away from the other children, correcting her favorite playmate's faulty pronunciation. After a time, she did the same inside: She began to greet therapists when entering the room and took pride in the other child's improved speech ability. She started to use materials more appropriately, to take her productions home, and to make friends. At discharge, she had changed sufficiently to make reentry into a preschool and adjustment there possible.

However, Katy developed psychosomatic problems at age 7 and was readmitted, this time into individual therapy. Her parents seemed more concerned with this physical problem and more amenable to change, in turn permitting Katy to desert her withholding patterns. She was able to talk about her own feelings of anxiety and low self-concept in relation to her older brother (He is perfect) and her younger sister (She is so tiny and pretty). Apparently, her withdrawal from social interaction was more an expression of anxiety and fear of rejection than of negativism, as had been previously postulated.

WHY ACTIVITY THERAPY?

Carefully selected activities provide learning experiences, social-interaction opportunities, and avenues for nonverbal expression of feelings. They offer the teacher and the therapist a multitude of insights into the intellectual, emotional, and physical level of operation of the child (Schaefer, 1976). Patterns of children's play, their drawings, their block building, the books they select—yes, all daily activities—help us to understand their earlier traumas, the models to which they have been exposed, and the problem-solving and conflict-resolution approaches they have learned and now need to unlearn. Children are extremely perceptive and follow the models provided for them, even if painful. They repeat the tone and the words of a chiding mother with uncanny accuracy.

When specific events are acted out repeatedly, they provide the therapist with opportunities for significant interventions. Young children are more willing to explore their fears and anxieties in a nonverbal fashion. But activities also reveal skills and interests, abilities and strengths. Imaginative play, be it in the doll house or the garage, helps the therapist to understand events originating in the family system and their impact on the child. Activities thoughtfully chosen to meet the needs of a child with specific problems might provide the experiences required to raise self-esteem, establish trust in helpful adults, and create a new world for the child.

Activities offer success experiences in a variety of areas and on the child's level. Demanding verbalization of problems at the preschool level is unrealistic. Children's anxieties, fears, wishes, and desires become apparent in their play activities, their choices of play materials, and their playmates. Age-appropriate, well-planned programming helps the therapeutic process.

Leslie, age 4, was referred to The Children's Center by her mother on the suggestion of her day-care teacher. Leslie was aggressive toward the other children and noncompliant toward adults. She has an older brother and an older sister; her parents divorced a year before she was referred.

Psychological evaluation showed Leslie to be a child of average intelligence with particularly good language skills. Projective instruments revealed concerns about abandonment, anger at males, a low self-concept, and poor play skills.

Staff questioned her need to be at the Center. Therapists felt she was a great model in the group and rewarded her behavior. During the second week, Leslie frequently asked the therapists at the end of the day if everybody was going to return the next day—the first indication of her earlier shown fear of abandonment. At the beginning of the third week, Leslie followed the example of another girl in the group and refused to come in from the playground. When the girls came in ten minutes later, they had missed snack but were greeted pleasantly. Leslie was surprised and appeared almost disappointed that no punishment ensued.

In the weeks following, Leslie began to play with the other children and slowly became a member of the group. Noncompliance on her part appeared limited to direct requests, such as cleaning up, coming in, or putting boots on, indicating her need for autonomy in decision making. When the therapists recognized this and offered choices to her that were acceptable within the framework of the group, her negative behavior notably diminished.

Leslie had developed a positive relationship with one of the therapists and was ready for processing of her behavior and using different media for expression of negative feelings. Her parents had also been in counseling at The Children's Center. Discussion with her parents and day-care workers revealed improvement at daycare and at home. Leslie was discharged from treatment after eight months, well able to assume leadership with peers and handle controversy with adults in a verbal manner. By treating Leslie and her parents, changes were made faster and further pathology was avoided. Treatment of the parents alone would most likely have dealt with the trauma of divorce and the child's problems would have been forgotten.

Inappropriate behavior patterns that develop at home generalize to larger circles like preschool or daycare. They become intensified and have additional ramifications, influencing social interactions with peers and other adults besides family members. These sequelae can be prevented by early intensive intervention using play activities in a group setting. Leslie learned to give up her antisocial behavior patterns through interaction with adults who encouraged autonomy and peers who modeled alternative behaviors for her.

The case material presented in the previous pages shows the eclectic nature of the model developed at The Children's Center. It is based on a combination of developmental, psychodynamic, and behavioral theories.

DEVELOPMENTAL THEORIES

The major developmental theoreticians agree that normal development presupposes successful negotiations of the challenges of one developmental stage as a prerequisite for healthy progression to the next stage. Children crawl before they walk, walk before they run, make large circles before they can make tiny ones. They are dependent before they can become independent, and they babble before they talk. Development is a continuous process; for example, the separation-individuation phase, most important at age two, reappears during adolescence. In their extensive research studies on temperament and development A. Thomas and S. Chess (1977) discovered that "a child expressed the same temperamental pattern at different ages, at each succeeding stage of development, in qualitatively different situations and experiences" (p. 28). Temperamental traits per se will not lead to deviant behavior patterns, but they might, in interaction with features of the environment, result in inappropriate adaptation and disruption of mastery of a developmental phase.

Mary, age 3, was referred to The Children's Center by her preschool teachers. Though she had been in the same group with the same children and teachers for three months, she cried daily when her mother dropped her off. Attempts to comfort her, leave her alone, or interest her in toys were not successful in changing her behavior. The family was puzzled because Mary had been a curious and independent child. A developmental history revealed that three months prior to entering preschool her mother had had an emergency operation necessitating a prolonged hospital stay. Mary had been cared for by loving grandparents, but she developed sleeping and eating problems. When her mother returned home, Mary's sleeping and eating problems disappeared, but Mary became hesitant to leave her backyard and clung to her mother.

Reconstructing the time frame of her mother's illness revealed that the significant separation had disrupted the process of separation-individuation (Mahler, 1972) and thus hindered progress to the next stage. Mother and Mary were seen jointly for a few play therapy sessions during which they played out Mother's leaving, Mary's anxiety about it, and her mother's return. Mary remained in preschool and was slowly able to regain her earlier confidence and autonomy.

Arrested developmental patterns indicated that the preceding stage had not been successfully completed, so further normal developmental progress was difficult and could not be achieved. Taking a developmental perspective permits us to view emotional problems with greater optimism, for arrested processes can be changed through the active participation of the child and alterations in the environment (Cooper and Wanerman, 1977).

Cultural differences rather than deficits within developmental patterning need to be considered. Had Mary come from a different environment, from a family of extended caretakers, a less-pronounced reaction to her mother's absence would have been expected. It is, therefore, important to view maladaptive behavior and mastery of developmental stages within the framework of the child's environment.

Unawareness or lack of full consideration of the child's environment might easily lead to an unwarranted diagnosis of pathology.

The major influence in the environment of the young child is the parent. Studies in temperament, particularly those by Thomas and Chess (1977), have led to the concept of a child's "goodness of fit," which refers to a match between child and parental characteristics. A "poor fit" of one child might necessitate "parental adaptations" for positive development of that child. This concept is very helpful in explaining to parents the existence of one disturbed child in a sibling group. However, the realization of having a "difficult" child should not keep parents from referring that child for treatment; in the course of therapy, everybody in the family can learn to adjust to individual differences.

Awareness of developmental states is very important for parents and all professionals working with young children. Participation of the parent in therapeutic reconstruction of disturbed relationships is essential when dealing with young children, and it is one of the important aspects of The Children's Center model. Traumatic interruption within a phase and lack of age-appropriate functioning within the child's immediate family or in the wider circle of preschool or daycare justify referral for treatment in a therapeutic environment.

How does a parent, teacher, or day-care worker recognize the need for therapeutic intervention? The difference between normal and disturbed behavior is one of degree, not of kind. It is a question of duration and intensity. All two-year-olds have temper tantrums, but if they happen several times a day and last for half an hour each, both parent and child need help. Such behavior is exhausting for both of them and demands intervention before it hinders progress in the child's development and keeps the parent from enjoying the child. A three-year-old's sleeping problem, whether it means two hours of bedtime or nap routines or refusing to sleep in his or her own bed, might be an indication of the child's need to control the family. On examination, there may appear other control issues, such as insisting on being first when playing with peers, sitting in the same spot at mealtime, and eating only certain foods. Giving in to these control issues will lead to the child's inability to compromise later on and to the parents' increasing frustration. Group therapy can be very helpful in these situations, as modeling by peers is at times much more impressive than an adult's intervention. Counseling with parents is essential; otherwise the children will triumphantly maintain their control at home.

Our society demands quite a bit from a four-year-old: good attending skills in church, an adequate vocabulary, completed toilet training, interest in peers, conflict resolution in a nonphysical way, and the ability to express affection spontaneously. Nonfunctioning on an age-appropriate level in any one of these areas might lead to trouble.

PSYCHODYNAMIC THEORIES

The Children's Center's treatment model is, to a large degree, based on psychodynamic theory. Since its inception in the early twentieth century, psychodynamic theory has undergone many changes that have made it more useful in therapeutic work with children (Biber, 1984, pp. 242, 292). Whereas earlier writers stressed the importance of instinctual drives, Anna Freud (1946) emphasized the ego as the main force in a child's development. The ego is generally understood to be the balance beam between the child's wishes and the values of society. If it is poorly developed and weak, the child will be in conflict with society and the environment. Although the infant is justified in seeking immediate gratification, such as food, as a life-saving device, delayed gratification must become part of the child's emotional equipment. That means waiting for a ride on the trike, not always being first in line or getting the largest piece of pie. It is up to the ego to perform the task of arbiter—not to be so strong that spontaneity is lost and societal values totally overshadow individual desires, or so weak that behavior is in opposition to established norms. Most children referred for treatment lack ego strength and need to lean on the therapist's ego during the process of strengthening their own. This process is gradual and depends to a large degree on the therapeutic alliance formed between therapist and child. This concept of developing ego strength fits well with the developmental theory of growth in separation-individuation. During this developmental phase, children become better able to handle complex situations as growth in ego strength occurs simultaneously.

Frederick Allen (1942) was one of the first to stress the necessity of building a positive self-image through a significant relationship with the therapist. He believed in the ability of the child to participate in the helping process, thus changing the pessimistic outlook of orthodox psychologists.

Erik Erikson (1950) is undoubtedly best remembered for his original work on the importance of psychosocial stages in development. Inclusion of the influence of the environment on emotional development and of positive and negative components in each stage has added to the usefulness of his theoretical paradigm, which is one of the cornerstones of the therapeutic model at The Children's Center. Most of the children we see totally distrust their environment, and change is not possible until trust is established. Development of trust, through acceptance of the children, understanding of their earlier experiences, consistency, and provision of success experiences, is the most important step in our therapeutic model.

Selma Fraiberg's (1987) discussion on attachment and bonding has major significance for work with young children. Those who show early signs of emotional disturbance have missed the secure attachment needed for normal development and age-appropriate functioning. They suffer in many instances from "the disease of nonattachment." This hinders their ability to form relationships and leads to disorders of impulse control and lack of conscience development. Again, the therapist in our treatment model acts as a positive attachment figure and thus tries to make up for such an earlier deficit.

Haim C. Ginott's (1976) concept of limit setting has influenced our work with emotionally disturbed preschoolers. We consider limit setting productive and essential for children with no internal control system. Limits help children look upon the therapist as a security figure who saves them from getting into trouble. For many children, this is a new experience that leads to positive identification with the therapist.

Limits direct unacceptable behavior into acceptable channels by symbolic means. The therapists can remain calm and accepting of the child if they set limits on the child's destructive behavior. It is important for the therapist to represent society to the children and to teach them the difference between acceptable and unacceptable behavior. It would also be impossible to handle groups of disturbed children without the setting of limits. Even Virginia Axline (1964, p. 242), a nondirective therapist, agrees that total permissiveness is not helpful in group situations, though she maintains this practice in individual sessions. Limits are also necessary for the safety of children and the therapist. Destructiveness or damage to the therapist creates guilt feelings that are contraindicated in a therapeutic relationship.

Although other dynamic theoreticians have made significant contributions, we have discussed only those whose work is particularly applicable to young children.

The Life Space Interview (LSI) technique, Fritz Redl's contribution to child therapy, has two major goals: "clinical exploitation of life events, and emotional first aid on the spot" (1966, p. 42). His method is widely used with preschoolers, latency-age children, and adolescents in many clinical settings and schools.

BEHAVIORAL THEORIES

A totally different psychological concept was developed by B. F. Skinner (1974). Based on observable behavior and conditioning, it has found widespread application in working with children. Behaviorists postulate that all behavior is learned through rewards and reinforcements. Therefore, it can be unlearned by the same method. For example, if a child always gets a toy in the store, he or she will demand a toy every time a visit to a store is made. Or if the child had a bad experience at the doctor's office, he or she will cry even when driving by. The use of rewards and reinforcements is an effective method to change behavior, though it is not quite as simple as imagined. If doing the right thing, doing what is expected, is consistently rewarded by parents, teachers, and society at large, such reinforcement will be habit forming, and the child will routinely perform in the desired way. In time the child will internalize positive behaviors, and a reward system will become unnecessary. In most of our lives, however, such regimentation is not possible. Unacceptable behaviors are not reinforced and, as the child longs for approval and rewards, the negative behaviors will be discarded. Consistency and careful observation of behaviors to be reinforced are essential for this method to have the desired effect.

Not all inappropriate behaviors can be remedied by behavioral techniques, just as not all aches and pains can be cured by Tylenol. Mary's crying, which prevented her social adjustment in preschool, needed to be understood from an interpersonal relationship-oriented paradigm. Observing her behavior and instituting a reward system, regardless of how sophisticated, might have alleviated the immediate behavior, but clinical experience has shown the reward system's later short-lived effects.

Why do some children refuse to be toilet trained? Is it a lack of developmental readiness or the desire to create a control issue with a parent? These questions need to be asked by parents, therapists, teachers, and pediatricians.

Behavioral techniques might take care of the observable behavior, but the question still remains: Why do the children select this specific behavior out of their total repertory of responses? For those answers we have turned with good success to the interpersonal relationship concepts discussed earlier. Through assessment techniques we learn about the child's emotional functioning and the family's strengths and weaknesses. The child's use of defenses, ability to delay gratification, and risk taking, as well as the family's commitment to treatment, are considered in developing a treatment plan using the most effective intervention techniques. Behavioral techniques, psychodynamic concepts, cognitive reasoning techniques, and reality-based natural consequences are used in different phases of treatment.

For all the team members to respond appropriately to the children's needs, those needs must be understood. Awareness of developmental states in cognitive, physical, and emotional areas is important for therapists, child-care workers, teachers of young children, and volunteers. Most professionals working with children, as well as parents, seem to be aware of physical milestones, but they find the steps in emotional development less clear. The next chapter highlights some theories that have been most useful in understanding this progression.

Chapter 2
Developmental Theories

INTRODUCTION

Developmental concepts cover a larger area than just achievements at certain age levels. Developmental psychologists are concerned with emotional stages in relationship to important figures in the children's environment and their impact on later personality development. Clinical psychologists need to be aware of children's emotional and social development because they usually work with children who show maladaptive patterns in that area. Teachers focus more generally on achievements in cognitive areas and only secondarily on social and emotional development.

At certain times in the history of child development and education, definite lines of demarcation were drawn between a child's intellectual functioning and social and emotional functioning. Fortunately, this tendency has disappeared to a large extent. The influence of one upon the other has been realized, and this has led to better understanding of children's lives. Professionals working in preschool education first recognized the significance of including environmental factors in a comprehensive developmental view. The Head Start Program, which was called the "enemy of family life" at its inception in 1950, has increased the awareness that the disadvantages of growing up under conditions of poverty can significantly affect later cognitive achievement.

The developmental-interactive approach (Biber, 1984) combines cognitive developmental approaches with Erikson's psychosocial formulations. During the early years, children's egocentricity greatly influences their view of the world and relationships to people. Many special-needs children remain in this egocentric stage, which hinders their cognitive as well as psychosocial functioning. During later preschool years, most children look at the world more objectively.

The developmental-interactive approach "favor[s] educational principles that are process- rather than product-oriented" (Biber, 1984, p. 301). When presented in connection with stage-specific psychosocial characteristics, cognitive activities will yield better results. Such an approach leaves ample room for creativity, curiosity, and development of a positive self-concept.

The model developed at The Children's Center encompasses such a developmental-interactive approach. Its focus is children who at an early age show non-age-appropriate functioning due to discrepancies between cognitive and social-emotional development. The same model can be used for children in the early grades within the public school system to address these discrepancies, which can otherwise lead to school drop out, unemployment, and antisocial behaviors.

Emotional upheaval is considered normal (Murphy, 1963) when it relates realistically to a situation, when the child can take care of it, or if it is transitory. Smooth progress is unlikely; ups and downs have to be accepted. In fact, many experts agree that phases of development are often preceded by crises, as if the organism is getting ready for a new growth spurt. Normal development depends on maturational processes and a facilitating, appropriate environment. Trouble can start if children have organic deficits, if their "timetable" is off, or if the environment is not an optimal or even adequate facilitator.

DEVELOPMENTAL EXPECTATIONS

If one is unaware of intellectual, physical, and emotional milestones, or of temperamental differences, an appropriate behavior might be labeled pathological. Being clear about developmental expectations at specific age levels is particularly important when working with young children, for children learn an enormous amount during the early years (i.e., from birth to age five). Unaware of developmental steps, parents and professionals frequently expect performance on an advanced level. This may have several consequences: The adult expects too much, sees failure, and shares that feeling with the child either through words or by action. Or the adult does not expect enough of the child, commenting repeatedly that he or she is not ready for a task. Both attitudes undermine the child's positive self-concept, leading to feelings of helplessness and anger, to oppositional behavior, and to a loss of self-confidence and initiative.

Ben, age 4, needed to use the bathroom during an evaluation session. A few minutes later he came out of the bathroom with his overalls unbuttoned and at his ankles. Mother, who was in the waiting room rushed to him saying, "Let me do it, honey," and turning to the examiner said, "I always do this for him."

Mary, 5 years, 6 months of age, was reading in kindergarten and the teacher suggested that she be advanced to first grade. Mary developed "morning" stomach aches on weekdays and did not want to go to school.

Regardless of how many charts are consulted or how much research is examined, each child is different. Combinations of genes and temperament create individual timetables. Children go through stages of development at their own rate and in a particular style.

GENERALLY ACCEPTED MILESTONES

Self-Care Skills

Two-year-olds begin to take interest in doing things for themselves. Self-care skills become a challenge for parents and toddlers. They try to zip, eat with a spoon, and undress readily. These skills gradually advance each year until by kindergarten age children are self-sufficient in dressing, eating, and toileting. Buttoning and lacing depend on small-motor coordination and often prove very difficult for cerebral palsy children and others with physical disabilities.

Intellectual Milestones

Cognitive achievements in two-year-olds have delightful results. Their receptive language, for example, understanding requests, responding to their own names, and repeating words, has blossomed. They can differentiate body parts and match simple shapes, and they take great delight in looking at and recognizing pictures of themselves and their caretakers. They learn by repetition and occupy themselves by building towers, knocking them down, and rebuilding them again, and by pouring water in and out of a container. By age three, children follow two-part directions, match primary colors, know their names, and listen to stories for ten minutes. Expressive language is clearer. They are eager to learn new words and use them, and they delight in rhymes. By age four, children can match pictures, participate in storytelling, and differentiate between one and many. They understand opposites and follow three-part directions. They use complete sentences and have a greatly enlarged vocabulary. Children are beginning to write their names and realize their gender. By age five, children respond to opposite analogies, reason, understand natural consequences, and are eager to learn. They talk constantly, like to tell stories, and ask where words come from. They like to learn languages other than their native one.

Physical Achievements

Two-year-olds walk and run, jump, and ascend stairs; pick up small items like peas; and hold a crayon in palmer grip. Three-year-olds ride trikes, stand on one foot for a second, use alternate feet to walk upstairs, string beads, hold a cup by the handle, and like to scribble. The four-year-old is very active, is sure footed, likes to throw a ball, begins to draw recognizable objects, and holds crayons in a pincer grip. The five-year-old moves arms and legs in unison, skips, plays ball, can write his or her name, copies a square, and cuts on lines and likes to do it.

Social and Emotional Characteristics

Two-year-olds show independence; they are assertive and want things right now; and they are eager, observant, open to ideas, and determined. They are attached to their mother or caregiver, slow to warm up to strangers, sensitive to loud noises, and fearful of thunder. They like sameness and often object to changes. Three-year-olds like to please; they are friendly, imaginative, and interested in peers. Adventurous, they like to do different things and to go places. They like to make choices and enjoy being with other children. Four-year-olds are creative sometimes in a negative way, expect much from themselves, are easily frustrated, and become aggressive when failing. Behavior varies greatly from day to day. Five-year-olds settle down again, show initiative, form close friendships, have a sense of humor, love to tell silly jokes, can give in, are close to both parents, and like to plan activities and trips.

In addition to these milestones, temperamental differences must be considered when evaluating children's age-appropriate functioning.

TEMPERAMENTAL DIFFERENCES

In their important book on temperament and development, Thomas and Chess (1977) discussed the historical tendency to blame maladaptive functioning of young children totally on their environment, and particularly on mothers. The most extreme example of "mother bashing" was the term *refrigerator mother*, applied to mothers of autistic children. The serious difficulties such children have were put squarely on the shoulders of the environment created by their mothers. Fortunately, this concept has disappeared, and with growing understanding and intensive therapeutic intervention, children with autistic features can make major progress (Greenspan, 1992).

An extensive, longitudinal research program by Thomas and Chess (1977) has uncovered the importance of temperamental inborn tendencies that need to be recognized by parents, teachers, and mental health workers in the evaluation of children. Thomas and Chess defined temperament as the *way* in which individuals behave, creating their own behavioral style. They established nine categories of temperament, which remain stable during each successive stage of development. Factor analysis of the data has shown that certain constellations of developmental traits differentiate groups of children. The difficult child, the slow-to-warm-up child, and the easy child represent variations within normal limits. It is an important concept for parents, teachers, and mental health workers to keep in mind. Temperamental traits must be considered in the context of environmental and ethnic influences but should not be overlooked when children with special needs are being considered for services. Temperamental characteristics can clarify a child's "fit" in the family system.

A strongly research-based theory of cognitive development (Piaget, 1983) has important implications for curriculum development. In the sensorimotor stage (birth to two years), the child deals with reality, whereas during the preoperational and operational stages (two to seven years), reality is combined with abstraction.

EMOTIONAL DEVELOPMENT

Erik Erickson (1950) formulated eight stages of the human life cycle, the first four of which are particularly significant to an understanding of the healthy emotional development of young children (David Elkind, 1970).

The first stage, *trust vs. mistrust,* takes place during the first year of life. Basic trust is established by meeting the infant's needs and by the quality of care it receives. Trust shows itself in the infant's ease of feeding, good sleeping patterns, and ability to be close to significant adults. The child learns to look at the world as a safe place, where he or she will be taken care of. If needs are not met or are met inconsistently, mistrust of others and of self develops. Fear of abandonment and lack of positive expectations indicate mistrust arising again later and forming a pattern of suspicion and anxiety.

Jonathan was 3 years old when first brought to The Center. Small and pale, he observed the world with large brown eyes that seemed to look through rather than at you. He would not enter the group therapy room, although encouraged by some of the children and invited by the therapist. He spent the first day mostly in the hall, and it took several weeks until he convinced himself that the same adults, the same children, and the same toys would be there. His mistrust was based on earlier experiences of changing caretakers, neglect, hunger, and fear.

Overcoming mistrust in young, emotionally deprived children frequently starts at this basic level and proceeds only slowly to the development of an emotionally trusting relationship, essential for further healthy development and a therapeutic alliance. It demands a consistency in the therapeutic milieu, the emotional availability of the therapist, and an understanding of the child's background, developmental level, and ego strength.

The establishment of basic trust helps the child to accept delayed gratification, develop a good feeling about the caregiver, and have positive self-esteem. "I am important enough to be taken care of" is a needed basis for future development. A parallel process goes on in the caregiver, usually the mother, which leads her to trust in her "good motherliness."

The basic issue of trust versus mistrust recurs at other stages of development. Frequent changes in caregivers, divorce, and abandonment resurrect the original crisis.

If the first stage has been successfully conquered, the child proceeds to the second stage between the ages of one and three. Erickson labeled this stage *autonomy vs. shame and doubt*. Once the child walks, runs, and climbs, independence is his or her major goal; The world is the child's oyster, so to speak, to explore and to experience. Children must be permitted to do everything they are capable of doing themselves because such freedom will give them a sense of control and, ultimately, of autonomy.

Mobility encourages exploration, but this newfound freedom has dangers, including the possible loss of love if exploration arouses the ire of caregivers. They may feel threatened by the child's newly discovered adventurous nature and independence.

Children often look at the caretaker while engaged in new and possibly nonapproved behaviors. The look is for reassurance that acceptance of themselves, though not necessarily of the behavior, is there. Independence is exhilarating, but scary. Children need to feel that a source of comfort is available and their exploration is appreciated. Once this feeling is internalized, exploration does not create anxiety, and true autonomy is established. Peek-a-boo games are favorites during this period, as the children learn the give and take of "here" and "gone."

The caretaker has to be ready to permit, yes, even encourage, the child to explore, for the consequences of denying such experimentation are longlasting. Mixing sugar and salt when nobody is looking might lead to an inedible cake, but it is not a catastrophe, just as asking for soup at breakfast is not a crime, only a Chinese custom. Disallowing all unorthodox behavior might easily lead to the child's self-doubt, and even shame if handled punitively. On the other hand, too much autonomy too early can produce a "tyrant in the house," one who pushes to make all the decisions and rules in the household. Such power is frightening for a young child and leads to unreasonable demands and inappropriate behaviors.

Tyrants at home demand their rights in inappropriate ways, since their approach is always based on the premise that they will not succeed. Their irrational demands, like staying up late or wearing the same T-shirt for a week, are often based on earlier unhappy experiences with rigid rules. They become fixated on achieving their goals aggressively and immediately, which hampers their future healthy development and creates problems in relationships.

Part of this struggle for autonomy is the child's need to experience the consequences of saying no. Will the caretaker become angry, punish, or not care? Children react differently depending on their temperamental makeup. Some will throw in the sponge and give up independence, exploration, and autonomy. They become overly dependent and anxious, avoid other children, and frequently show symptoms of depression. Many of these children are not referred for treatment as preschoolers as they appear to be so good. Often they do not attend preschool or daycare, and intervention is sought only when they enter school and are not performing. Then the "goodness" is questioned.

In the best scenario, the no will be accepted and recognized as a stepping stone; appropriate compromises will be made, choices given, and alternatives suggested. Spending time with parents, preschool teachers, and therapists able to accept the child's emerging autonomy and praise it or handle it constructively will help diminish the confusion between "Is it okay to be independent?" and "Will I lose love by doing my own thing?"

Other children will react with strongly negative behaviors, pushing for their autonomy regardless of the consequences. These might well be children whose development of trust had been tentative, who now again question trust in adults, and who use autonomy as the next arena for challenging the adult's control. They react with exaggerated negative behavior, and home becomes a battleground.

Martin, a 4-year-old only child from an intellectual, upper-middle-class family, was referred by his preschool teacher. He was isolated and mute in preschool, demanding and aggressive at home. He observed the children but did not enter into group activities. Consultation revealed that Martin was the product of an unwanted premarital pregnancy. He was still in diapers at night and given a bottle on demand. Entering the outside world revealed his excessive sense of doubt and shame about his own abilities and his impotence to control the world. Withdrawal at preschool and anger at home were his only means of expressing his unhappiness.

Empathy and thoughtfulness during this phase will make "the terrible two's" a challenge, but not a battleground. Children are often not referred for treatment at this time, partly because parents do not understand their involvement in the process and are waiting for the phase to go away and for the child to change on his or her third birthday. Referrals are made most commonly when the behavior causes concern outside of the home environment, in preschool, daycare, or church.

Successful accomplishment of the two previous stages is a prerequisite for further age-appropriate development. *Initiative vs. guilt* is the next stage, reached by the age of four or five. Freedom from fear of risking and a positive self-concept encourage self-initiated activities. When parents and caregivers accept new ideas, answer questions, and laud new motor activities, they strengthen the child's initiative and establish a sense of excitement for the future. If questions are labeled as silly and physical activity devalued, the child may develop a sense of guilt over self-initiated activities.

Entering kindergarten, children approach the fourth stage in development. Erickson labels this stage *Industry vs. inferiority.* Children learn to use tools and find out how things are made, how they work, and what they can do. Achievement becomes important, and the sense of industry is strengthened if children are encouraged to make useful objects—such as a bird feeder or Jell-O for dinner. School experiences strongly determine success. Wrong classroom placement of a gifted or slow child may create a sense of inferiority. Playing games by rules becomes a challenge, and relationship to peers increases in importance.

Erikson's stages are useful in understanding the young child. Other theories, like those of Mahler (1972) on individuation-separation and the formulations of Bowlby (1988) and Ainsworth and others (1979) on attachment, are needed to understand the emotional development of children.

Mahler assumes the existence of a symbiotic unit between mother and child from the first to the fifth months after birth. The child is unaware of distance between itself and its mother; hence, attachment is a given. Individuation-separation is a struggle, one of breaking away for the child and one of letting go for the mother. During this differentiation process, the child moves away from the mother, using her for emotional refueling and gaining independence confidently if it is provided.

At this point, children can walk, explore their surroundings, and feel increasingly omnipotent. Such independent action develops mastery and confidence, but it also raises separation anxiety and confusion in the child. He or she wants to be independent but becomes easily frustrated and oppositional, demanding considerable understanding from parents. If this is not forthcoming, there develop behavior patterns that might lead to later pathology. Some children remain arrested in their earliest independence phase, developing controlling behaviors, while others remain overly dependent, fearing loss of love. The child's realization of gender differences also occurs at this time, adding to confusion and anxiety.

Mahler's theory puts heavy responsibility on both parents, but particularly on mother. Many teenage mothers and those who have grown up in dysfunctional families themselves have great difficulties fulfilling the role ascribed to them by Mahler. In many cases, children referred to The Children's Center have not satisfactorily managed the individuation-separation phase. Intervention at an early age can make up for this deficit when the therapist substitutes for the missed dyadic relationship and allows the child to work out the conflict in a more neutral, less emotionally charged context.

Bowlby and Ainsworth described attachment as an emotional bond that develops between an infant and its caregiver during the first year of life. An attachment figure is someone for whom the child develops a preference and to whom it turns for comfort when frightened or distressed. Bowlby placed particular emphasis on the importance of physical contact for establishing and maintaining attachment relationships. Attachment to the mother, or caregiver, is viewed as primary, not as a derivative of her role as a need-gratifier. Once formed, attachment relationships continue to play an important role throughout the life span. Development is not viewed as progressing from a state of dependency to independence; rather, growing confidence in the caregiver's availability and responsiveness leads to emotional security and allows the child to maintain a healthy balance between self-reliance and reliance on others.

Bowlby was among the first to draw attention to the process of grief and mourning in infants and young children. Prolonged separation from, or loss of, an attachment figure during childhood leads to anxiety, anger, depression, and emotional detachment.

Molly, barely 3, and her five siblings were placed in a foster home after their mother's violent death. All the children had been previously removed from their home due to neglect.

Molly's behavior in group as well as with her individual therapist was one of initial clinging and subsequent withdrawal. She had a difficult time relating to her peers.

Ainsworth has extended Bowlby's work on separation and loss by showing that a parent's emotional availability and responsiveness on a daily basis are critical to the child's security. Children whose parents respond sensitively to their needs form secure attachments to them, whereas children who receive highly interfering, rejecting, or neglectful care form insecure attachment relationships. Expectations and ways of relating learned in these first relationships carry over to new encounters.

Johnny, age 4, was referred for treatment because he consistently ran away from his foster homes. At the time of admission, he had been in five foster homes since his teenage mother abandoned him at age 2. He wandered into malls and walked off with strange females. Placement in The Children's Center's residential group home for a year, followed by individual therapy in an adoptive home over a two-year period, helped him to attach and bond. Running away was the observable symptom; the lack of early bonding, the true reason for the behavior.

Consideration of these different theories provides a basis for intervention strategies with young, emotionally disturbed children. In summary, optimal conditions for healthy emotional development are based on attachment to a mother or consistent caregiver who provides security, permits individuation, separation, and autonomy, but remains available as an agent for emotional refueling. Many children lack such early experiences and are a challenge to teachers and mental health professionals. The sooner such attachment figures can be provided, the faster normal development can proceed.

Anni, age 4, was referred by her pediatrician because she had demolished his office during her last visit. She was the only girl in a family of five children and was in a middle ordinal position. The family was delighted with her gender and tried with consecutive pregnancies to even out the home team. However, this did not materialize, and Anni was expected to fill the role of the dainty, polite, feminine child. As it turned out, she was more athletic than her next older brother, taller and more muscular. The lacy pink dresses did not please her; she lived in jeans and T-shirts, to the displeasure of the extended family. Anni was angry that she was different, said openly she would like to be a boy, and related better to her father than to her mother.

Family study revealed that the family system perpetuated male domination. Mother felt overburdened and put in her place; she did not like it, but she did not rebel in even the slightest way. Anni never needed treatment on her own. Once the perpetuating element was removed, Anni's abilities were recognized, her mother returned to college, and her older brother was permitted to take a summer art class rather than join the soccer team.

The correlation of specific steps with certain age levels is generally acknowledged, but genes and environment affect this progression.

Barbara Kalmanson (1989) (see Appendix A) has developed a scheme of developmental vulnerabilities based on particular domains of development. They are helpful in determining whether difficulties are pervasive and demand intervention. If the child's timetable is off or the environment is not facilitating developmental progress, intervention is needed. Deficits hindering normal emotional and intellectual development need to be resolved. The final aim of intervention strategies is to help children solve conflict situations, not to avoid them. That goal can be reached in a number of different ways.

A schematic presentation of generally agreed behaviors at specific age levels is found in Appendix B. These are only general guidelines and to be used thoughtfully. These guidelines should also be considered when planning for treatment, which is discussed in detail in the next chapter.

Chapter 3
Planning for Treatment

INTRODUCTION

All children show inappropriate behaviors at one time or another. In the lives of disturbed children, however, these behaviors are more intense, appear more frequently, and last longer. It follows, then, that disturbed children are different not in kind but only in degree. Acceptance of such an attitude helps mental health workers, teachers, and parents to be optimistic about treatment outcome, and this optimism transmits itself to the children and the adults in contact with the children.

Children are referred to treatment agencies or special services within the school system because they have shown inappropriate behaviors. These can be externally directed, like aggression toward peers, noncompliance, and the pushing of limits in one-to-one situations with authority figures. They can also be internalized, like refusal to participate, selective muteness, depression, anxiety, attachment disorders, and eating and sleeping problems.

Referral concerns are frequently reported in general terms and based only on observable behavior and environmental circumstances. Careful initial evaluation procedures are essential for understanding of the child. These procedures should consist of psychological testing, including projective measures like storytelling tests and human figure drawing, in addition to measurements of cognitive abilities. Projective instruments discover underlying conflicts important for the development of a meaningful treatment plan. Not all children labeled aggressive are angry, not all overly active ones hyperactive, and not all withdrawn ones shy. Obtaining a careful developmental history sheds light on the child's accomplishments of physical, cognitive, and social-

Table 3.1
Intake Procedures

Phone Call From Parent

Intake Sheet Completed

Intake Staff Meeting

Psychological Evaluation → Parent/Child Consultation

Disposition

- Admission
  - Mother/Toddler Group
  - Outpatient Group
  - Day Rx
  - Short-term Parent Counseling
  - Parenting Class
- Referred Out
  - Mental Health Center
  - Private Practitioners
  - Interagency Coord. Council

emotional goals. The timing of the appearance of problems is considered, and family dynamics are explored.

Three important elements in treatment planning need to be carefully examined: (1) the predisposing element, such as constitution, temperament, ordinal position in the family, and physical handicaps; (2) the precipitating element, which is frequently overlooked, such as the arrival of a new sibling, separation or divorce, change of a babysitter, illness in the family, loss of a friend, or death of a pet; and (3) the perpetuating element, such as the preoccupation of the family with the child's symptom. The latter element fosters continuation of the inappropriate behavior and meets the psychological needs of one or the other family member.

Most referrals come to The Children's Center from parents on suggestion from social service agencies, former clients, and physicians. Proof of legal custody is requested from divorced families.

When the parents call, the secretaries record the name and date of birth of the child, referral source, previous contact with The Children's Center, names of parents (frequently different) and their addresses, phone numbers, and places of work.

This initial information is turned over to the clinical staff member on intake that day. This individual returns the phone call as soon as possible and completes the intake sheet (see Table 3.1). Further information, such as medical reports, reports from daycare, school reports, and legal documents, is requested, if germane. The source of funding is explored. The parent is referred to an administrative assistant to discuss fees if parents have insurance. Parents on Medicaid pay no fee because the Center has a contract with the State Mental Health Agency, which administers all Medicaid Services in the state, but parents must have proof of eligibility. Completion of the intake sheet by a clinical staff member is considered important, since it is the family's first involvement with the agency. Also, it frequently reveals the urgency of the situation and the family's commitment to treatment.

INTAKE STAFF MEETING

The staff meeting consists of two parts: discussion of new intakes and assignments, and disposition of evaluated cased. All intakes received during the week are reviewed at an intake meeting attended by psychiatrists, psychologists, social workers, and staff providing auxiliary services. Typical intakes during one week are shown in the following section.

Discussion of New Intakes

GIRL (5): Depressed and moody, very down but then has angry outbursts. Aggressive, gets picked on at school. Dad's in prison. Mom is overwhelmed and has financial problems.

GIRL (5): Keeps everything inside. Picks at her skin until she draws blood. Severe temper outbursts. Says, "I don't want to be beautiful." Parents getting divorced.

GIRL (6): Has been diagnosed ADHD (Attention Deficit Hyperactivity Disorder), PDD (Pervasive Developmental Disorder), or developmentally delayed. Has sensory-integration and auditory-processing problems. Violent, head banging; doesn't sleep.

BOY (5): Won't listen. Disregards authority figures. Argues until he gets his way.

BOY (4): Self-destructive, pinches and scratches himself. Won't listen, urinates on floor, aggressive toward brother, hyperactive.

BOY (4): Overreacts to everything, cries most of the time. Doesn't eat, won't talk, isolates. Afraid of going to knock on a friend's door. Parents recently separated—used to argue in front of kids.

BOY (4): Always on the move. Bolted out of the car and it took thirty minutes to find him. Won't respond to discipline. Extreme noncompliance. "Stop" doesn't register. Adopted at eight weeks; born addicted to cocaine.

BOY (3): Severely sexually abused by father. Now afraid of everything. Sees spiders when there aren't any.

BOY (3): Sexually abused by an adult male. Rectum was badly stretched. Now resists having diaper changed. Takes off diaper and fondles himself. Hits when he's angry.

GIRL (5): Always talking about death. Says, "I wish I'd die." "You want me dead." Won't accept any comfort. Abandoned by biological mother.

BOY (4): Vocabulary of less than thirty words. Stays with an activity only thirty seconds, won't sit still to look at a book. Five to six temper tantrums daily. Tried to stab baby with screwdriver, pokes mom and dad with knives, kicks and bites them.

BOY (2): Violent, bangs head, kicks and hits self. Violent toward peers. Doesn't talk. Severe tantrums.

BOY (5): Started fire in his house with a lighter. Says he wants to kill people. Doesn't listen to adults. Performed oral sex on a younger child. Beats his four-year-old brother and tried to drown him in the bath tub.

Assignments

Mother/Toddler Group

Outpatient Group

Psychological Evaluation
Parent/Child Consultation
Referral to Other Agencies

Referral to Mother/Toddler Group

Children between eighteen and thirty months of age are assigned to the therapists in charge of the mother-toddler program. Since it is not a therapeutic but an educational program, it is discussed under auxiliary educational programs.

Referral to Outpatient Groups

Children between the ages of five and seven are referred to outpatient groups. Each center conducts afterschool groups for five-, six-, and seven-year-olds. They meet twice a week for one and one-half hours for activity group therapy sessions. Nonfunctioning in school and lack of peer interaction are frequent referral concerns. Emphasis is on discussion of feelings, social skills, and conflict-resolution techniques. The groups are conducted by social workers and graduate students. Parents are seen in counseling sessions. Close cooperation with schools is maintained to provide a continuum of services.

Shane, age 5, was brought to the Center by his mother. He would not go to sleep until midnight, refused foods he had loved previously, and despite his superior intelligence, was "failing" in kindergarten.

Both parents were supported in discussing with Shane the reasons for their divorce, setting realistic limits on his behavior at home and in school, and reinforcing his many exceptional abilities. He was assigned to an outpatient group with a male therapist who could provide short-term, nonthreatening transitional first aid, and a female therapist who could absorb, interpret, and redirect some of Shane's unexpressed anger. The school's cooperation was obtained. Shane's nonparticipation in routine was overlooked, and creative ideas were reinforced. This increased his peer relationships and made use of his exceptional intellectual endowment. After a short time, sleeping and eating problems disappeared, relationship to his mother improved considerably, functioning in school became adequate, but Shane's ability to communicate with his father remained poor. We suspect that this will take individual psychotherapy when Shane reaches pre-puberty. (Plenk, 1978, p. 212)

Referral for Psychological Evaluation

A whole chapter is devoted to this topic.

Referral for Consultation

Referral is suggested when the problem has persisted for a limited time only, for example, less than two months. Sometimes precipitating elements, like the birth of a sibling, divorce, death of a significant adult, or the assumption of full-time employment by the caretaker, lead to disturbed behaviors. Consultation with the parent, a few individual meetings with them and the child, or admission to a different preschool or daycare center may alleviate the problem. In addition, this approach will give the parents a feeling of strength, having handled the situation themselves. This solution demands intuition and experience from the mental health worker.

Referral is also considered when there is conflict between parent and child but good adjustment in daycare, preschool, or school and with other adults. In this case conjoint sessions with parent and child in a playroom setting are helpful and, at times, quite readily reveal the source of the difficulty. It may be that expectation levels are developmentally too high, which will push some children into perfectionism and to being fearful of taking risks; or they may be too low, which encourages helplessness. Pinpointing the child's strengths and helping parents look at developmental stages might remedy the situation. Care must be taken, however, to not minimize the parent and the child's pain; and the door must be left open for further treatment.

Referral for Services at Other Agencies

At times children are referred to the Interagency Coordinating Council. The directors of the community's children's agencies (Head Start, Handicapped Preschool Classes, and The Children's Center) meet monthly to avoid duplication of services or, if necessary, provide full-day programming for children at high risk.

Referrals are also made to local mental health centers and private practitioners if the referrals do not appear appropriate for The Children's Center. Families already in treatment at mental health centers or those who have other children in treatment at local psychiatric facilities fall into this category.

Parents are notified by telephone of the assignments made, and appointments for psychological evaluations and consultations are scheduled and confirmed by letter.

Disposition of Evaluated Cases

After completion of the psychological evaluation and the consultation, cases are presented at staff meetings with recommendations for disposition. These recommendations fall into three categories: day treatment, short-term counseling, and no treatment–referral to parenting class.

Day Treatment

If admission to day treatment has been decided upon and a slot in a group is available, a group is selected and a therapist assigned to work with the parent. The psychologist meets with the parents to discuss the test results and recommendations. If parents agree, an admission date is set and the parents are introduced to the social worker who will be the case manager.

On admission day, parents and the child meet with the case manager, and together they take the child to group. Parents meet the child therapists and stay in the group for a little while, depending on the child's adjustment to the group. They then meet with the record clerk or bookkeeper to fill out papers needed for billing and for the transportation supervisor. The case manager sets a time for their first meeting, at which time the family history is taken.

During the first supervisory conference after admission, a treatment plan is formulated. It is based on the therapists' initial report, the psychological evaluation of the child, and the family history.

Treatment goals, written in behavioral, measurable terms, address the major problems reported by parents, observed by the child therapist, and identified through the psychological evaluation. Expressing a child's need in behavioral terms only is, at times, difficult; and a clinical formulation should always be attempted with the help of the family history obtained by the parent therapist (French, 1977). There are short-and long-term treatment goals: The immediate goal might, for example, be to help the child become more compliant to adult requests, while the long-term goal might be to increase feelings of trust that will lead to diminishing power struggles. Most children at The Children's Center lack adequate play skills, and one treatment goal usually refers to this lag.

Unfortunately, The Children's Center has a long waiting list for day treatment, at times necessitating a waiting period of several months. More and more frequently, due to the severity of the referral problems, parents are being seen in individual sessions or in a parenting group prior to the child's admission.

Short-Term Parent Counseling

Short-term parent counseling follows a consultation or the disposition meeting after a psychological evaluation. The clinician decides whether the family will be able to respond to suggestions and carry through behavioral assignments. Appropriate reading material is discussed in the sessions and sent home. Community facilities are brought to the parents' attention. The "problem" child, and at times the whole family, is included in issues aired. If a day-care situation brought the parent to the agency, the day-care outreach coordinator will visit, observe, make suggestions, or, if needed, indicate a change. Toy libraries, recreational facilities, and services provided by the Department of Human Services are called to the family's attention. Four or five weekly sessions are followed by a phone call to determine progress made.

No Treatment–Referral to Parenting Class

The no treatment–referral is a didactic six-session class held twice a year for parents whose children are not in treatment at The Children's Center. An outline of the material covered in this program follows in a later chapter.

The next chapter discusses the assessment of all aspects of the child's personality and the family's functioning prior to the onset of treatment. It is hoped that this assessment process convinces parents of the agency's concern and deepens their commitment to their child.

Chapter 4
Assessment

INTRODUCTION

Psychological evaluation of preschool children demands a great deal of flexibility in administration of standardized instruments, a basic understanding of developmental expectations, and, most of all, a genuine liking for children and their individual differences. The therapist needs to approach each child with an open mind as to the possible findings, rather than beginning an evaluation with a preconceived idea, conditioned by the referral concerns, of what the diagnosis will be. Sometimes observable behavior is a smoke screen, and the real reasons for the smoke need to be sensitively explored.

While validation and standardization of the instruments selected are certainly important, sensitivity to the child's feelings is essential. The child is meeting with a stranger—a "doctor," no less—in an unknown environment, possibly with some misconceptions. Doctors are frequently remembered unpleasantly by children, which makes the introduction to the psychologist a crucial one.

It is sometimes necessary to alleviate the parent's and the child's anxiety by giving them advice on how to prepare for a visit to a psychologist. The preparation the day before depends on the child's age and the referral concerns. Let us assume the child is three years old and has stopped going outside alone. The parent might say: "You have not been happy lately and don't play with the other children any more. We'll go see a lady (man) who will help you and mommy and daddy be happier. No, she (he) won't give you shots." A four-year-old who has set fire to his baby sister's crib needs to be told, "You did something very dangerous, and we all need to find out what made you so upset." In a case where the child knows about a pending divorce, the introduction needs to be specific: "There will be lots of changes, and we all need some help with them. Mom and dad will go, too, and while we talk you'll draw pictures and maybe play."

Pleasant physical surroundings, a colorful waiting room, smiling faces of receptionists, and a short or absent waiting period are helpful to make the child and family comfortable. The evaluation process is set in motion with the completion of the intake information sheet, which indicates the reasons for referral (see Table 4.1).

PSYCHOLOGICAL EVALUATION

Every psychological assessment begins in the waiting room (Adams, 1982) with observation of the parent-child interaction, their communication pattern, their appearance, and the child's activity level. Adjacent offices to be used for the parent interview and the testing are helpful, as they permit continued observation of the child's involvement in play, selection of play material, and ability to be separated from the parent or parents. These are important indicators of the child's adjustment.

Psychological assessments at The Children's Center consist of a developmental history, a test battery, a play interview, a test report, and a disposition meeting with the parents.

DEVELOPMENTAL HISTORY

The format of the developmental history might seem awkward, but it is organized to meet Medicaid requirements. The history is obtained from the parents to gain information regarding their major concerns about their child, the conditions of the mother's pregnancy and delivery, and the family's past and present constellation. The child's physical, social-emotional, and medical background is established, and motor milestones, self-care skills, and relationship to parents and peers are noted. Data are obtained concerning the forms of discipline used, the child's reaction to it, and current adaptive behaviors. Also recorded is the family's psychiatric history.

TEST BATTERY

Introduction

Psychological evaluations of preschool children need to consider the short timeframe of the child's attention span which, in certain respects, determines the selection of instruments. In addition to meeting

Table 4.1
The Children's Center
Intake Information Sheet

Date: <u>10/80</u>

Worker:_____

DAY RX____ OP ____

Child's Name: <u>Jimmy O.</u>   M/F   DOB: <u>10/20/75</u> Age: <u>4-0</u>

Who Called: <u>Mother</u>   Referred by: <u>T.V. PSA</u>

Prior Contacts with TCC: <u>No</u>   Pediatrician: <u>Dr. Blue</u>

Mother's Name: <u>Ann</u>   Phone: _____

Address: <u>XY Street</u>   Zip: _____

Employer & Job Title: _____ Work Phone: _____

Father's Name: <u>Ben</u>   Phone: _____

Address: <u>Same</u>   Zip: _____

Employer & Job Title: <u>Self</u>   Work Phone: _____

===

Other Parental Information: _____

MAJOR REFERRAL REASONS: <u>Poor attention, high activity</u>

<u>level. Trouble in neighborhood. Needs attention.</u>

<u>Controlling.</u>

Siblings & Ages: <u>sister (2), sister (1 month)</u>

Similar Problems with Siblings: <u>No</u>

How have you been handling these problems? _____

How long have these problems existed? _____

Any precipitating events? Changes? <u>Baby. Poor business.</u>

Previous treatment: <u>None</u>

Stressors in home: <u>New baby.</u>

Table 4.1 (continued)

What would you like from us? _____

Parents are: ___Living together _X_ Married ___Separated

___Divorced ___Widowed

Child lives with: <u>Parents</u>

Non-custodial parent's role/visitation: _____

Custody eval involved:_____

Where child is during day [Day Care (name), Home, Etc.):

<u>Snow White</u>

Teacher: <u>Betty</u>   Grade:_____   Phone:_____

Agencies currently involved with child or family: <u>None</u>

Reports requested from: _____

---

reliability and validity standards, they also have to be developmentally correct and challenging. The tests listed next in this chapter comprise the basic instruments used in evaluations at The Children's Center. One or two of the cognitive and visual-motor tests and all of the projective tests and the behavior checklists are routinely included in evaluations.

It is effective to begin with a cognitive measure such as the Stanford-Binet, as almost all children can pass one or the other subtest on their age level or the one below. This positive experience builds rapport that can then lead to the introduction of more difficult tasks.

TESTS USED

Measures of Cognitive Skills

Of the many intelligence tests available, the Center uses the following:

Nonverbal Children or Those under Age Two

Bailey Scales of Infant Development
Merrill-Palmer Scale of Mental Tests
Leiter International Performance Scale–Arthur Adaptation.

Children between the Ages of Two–Six, and Six

Stanford-Binet Intelligence–Fourth Edition
Stanford-Binet Intelligence Test, L-M

Children above Age Six

Wechsler Intelligence Scale for Children–Revised

Measures of Visual Motor Skills

Developmental Test of Visual-Motor Integration–Revised
Bender Gestalt Test

Measures of Social-Emotional Functioning

Projective Tests

Draw-A-Person Test
Draw-A-Family Test
Plenk Storytelling Test

Behavior Checklists

Achenbach Behavior Checklist
Parental Stress Inventory
Temperament Assessment Battery
Connors Parent Questionnaire

Measures of Language Skills

Peabody Picture Vocabulary Test

In addition, the following tests are administered by the speech pathologist:

Goldman-Fristoe Test of Articulation
Hresko, Reid and Hammill Test of Early Language Development
Spontaneous Language Sample
Tympanogram and Audiogram
Audiometric Pure Tone Screening Test

Measures of Cognitive Skills

Bailey Scales of Infant Development

The Bailey test is used only rarely, since we do not admit children under age two for treatment.

The Merrill-Palmer Scale of Mental Tests

The Merrill-Palmer is largely nonverbal and approximates non-discriminatory, culture-free testing. Unfortunately, the scoring system is rather dated; for example, the practice of allowing credit for refusals does not differentiate adequately between ability and emotional determinants.

Observation during administration of this test must be particularly keen, as it yields helpful clues for diagnosis and treatment. Children's task persistence, their ability to function under time pressure, and their approach to problem solving become apparent. The Merrill-Palmer is "intrinsically interesting to children; its face validity is excellent, and the variety of items quite appealing. Its three puzzles, for example, are unique, and so removed from most children's experience that no practice effects per se are expected" (Plenk and Hinchey, 1985, p. 132).

In our highly verbal society, lack of age-appropriate language skills is a serious handicap; and the discovery of cognitive, albeit nonverbal, strength in such children is reassuring to parents, as well as essential for a diagnosis and an appropriate treatment plan. Selected subtests of the Merrill-Palmer are also very helpful in "warming up" children for a more structured measure like the Stanford-Binet scales.

The Leiter International Performance Scale–Arthur
Adaptation

Developed for hearing-impaired children, the Leiter scale is also useful in testing non-English-speaking older children. It is quite difficult to administer, demanding dexterity on the examiner's part and patience on the child's. Again, new validation measures are needed; but, in the meantime, it is a helpful instrument.

The Stanford-Binet Intelligence Scales

The fourth edition of the Stanford-Binet Intelligence Scale (SB:IV), published in 1986, has not proven to be helpful with our at-risk population. Many children do not reach a basal level, quickly become discouraged, and give up. Preschoolers function best when immediately gratified, and advancing to the next area of subtests after several failures is not productive for them. R. R. Schnell and K. Workman-Daniels (1992) conclude in their detailed discussion of advantages and limitations of SB:IV, in comparison to earlier editions of the Stanford-Binet Intelligence Scale, that "the SB:IV subtest format does not appear to be as appealing to younger preschool children, as it is less flexible in format, requires longer administration time and has less variety of intrinsically interesting material" (p. 183). The higher floor level also limits its usefulness for younger preschoolers.

Because of these limitations of the fourth edition, the Center has returned to the use of the L-M edition if the child does not reach a basal level on SB:N. The test construction and the items used on the L-M version seem to measure our children's cognitive skill level well, except for a few outdated items.

Wechsler Intelligence Scale for Children–Revised

The revised Wechsler is used with children over age six. Schnell and Workman-Daniels (1992, p. 188) thoughtfully discuss instruments available for the intellectual assessment of preschoolers and conclude that much work remains to be done to achieve a really "relevant" instrument.

Measures of Visual-Motor Skills

The Developmental Test of Visual-Motor Integration (VMI)

Determination of children's visual-motor ability is important in the early detection of possible learning disabilities. The VMI presents structure within which designs are copied. This is helpful not only in the determination of the child's visual-motor ability, but also gives clues as to oppositional, noncompliant tendencies.

The Bender Gestalt Test

The Bender Gestalt is an important test instrument in the determination of possible neurological impairment and learning disabilities for children above the age of five. Children's different performances on the VMI and on the Bender are, at times, diagnostically significant.

Measures of Social-Emotional Functioning

Projective Tests

The use of projective tests in the clinical assessment of young children draws the sharpest line of demarcation between behaviorally and dynamically oriented psychologists. Hypotheses concerning the origin and intensity of children's emotional problems can sometimes be as productive as behavior assessment grids in understanding children. If a child has an age-appropriate score on the VMI but responds when asked to draw his family by producing *only* a perfect picture of a dog, one can assume some difficulty in interpersonal relationships. Despite harsh criticism (Knoff, 1992, pp. 138–139), projective tests seem here to stay.

The Draw-A-Person (DAP) and Draw-A-Family (DAF) tests give valuable information as to children's feelings about themselves and their position within the family system. Size, placement, and inclusion of family members tell a great deal about the confused world in which many at-risk children live. Young children seem to find it easier to express feelings visually, and these measures exploit this tendency. Greater visual acuity might be due to watching television.

Both human figure drawing tests can be useful in the discovery of sexual abuse. Preschoolers do not usually draw genitalia and label it, except in cases of sexual molestation or precocious interest in sexual matters. Research mentioned by A. Tyler and V. R. Gregory (1992, p. 380) indicates that the Human Figure Drawing Test can differentiate sexually abused children from emotionally disturbed and from well-adjusted children (Koppitz, 1968).

The Plenk Storytelling Test (PST)

The PST (Plenk, Hinchey, and Davies, 1985) was developed as an alternative to the Children's Apperception Test (CAT) (Bellak and Adelman, 1960), which shows animals performing human acts. The CAT, as well as the PST, demands identification with the stimulus material presented. Clinical practice has shown that young children at risk, particularly those not familiar with fantasy material, have difficulty identifying with nonhumans but readily become involved in producing stories with stimuli depicting everyday situations and human subjects. The nine PST pictures deal with scenes showing adult-child and child-child interaction, in conflict, and play situations. Interpretation can be based on a numerical scoring system, but the test is best used clinically rather than statistically.

Sexually and physically abused children often respond with explicit stories, but research is needed before projective tests will be legally acceptable in determination of sexual or physical abuse.

The material produced is scored in reference to conscience development, significant concerns, conflict resolution, trust in the world, and relationship to parental figures. Peer relationships, ability to express and accept feelings, and the child's view of the world become apparent in the stories. Pre- and post-testing with the PST is also useful as a measure of treatment progress.

"In discussing techniques and tools of projective assessment, it is essential that interpretation be made cautiously, and the caveat given that information elicited be viewed only in context with other data obtained in the assessment procedure" (Plenk, Hinchey, and Davies, 1985, p. 133). Much information concerning the child's social-emotional functioning can be obtained from rating scales completed by the parent(s) or caregiver(s) and from behavioral observations.

Rating Scales

Achenbach Behavior Checklist
Parental Stress Index
Temperament Assessment Battery Checklist
Connors Parent Questionnaire

The Achenbach Behavior Checklist (1983), the Parental Stress Index (1986), and the Temperament Assessment Battery (1988) are used for all children as a pre- and post-measure. The Connors Parent Questionnaire is used when indicated by observation or referral concerns. Although the data gained from some of the checklists are not always helpful in understanding the child, they yield valuable information about the parents' perception of their child's functioning and personality makeup.

Measures of Language Skills

The Peabody Picture Vocabulary Test–Revised

The Peabody test proves helpful in determining children's receptive language ability. Lack of or poor expressive speech does not necessarily reflect on children's ability to understand language and its usage. This test measures strengths useful in the rehabilitation of children who are not functioning age-appropriately. The Peabody Picture Vocabulary Test needs to be presented rapidly, as its structure of four pictures on a page easily overstimulates children. Many children, particularly those in speech therapy, are so eager to show off their newly acquired knowledge of words that they point to every picture, thus nullifying the measure. Practice effect needs to be taken into consideration when children are in speech therapy.

The following tests are administered by the speech therapist: Goldman-Fristoe Test of Articulation; Hresko, Reid, and Hammill Test of Early Language Development; Spontaneous Language Sample; Tympanogram and Audiogram; Audiometric Pure Tone Screening Test. The Spontaneous Language Sample is given to all children on admission. The Test of Early Language Development is given to children who had difficulty with the Goldman-Fristoe. The Tympanogram and the Audiometric Pure Tone Screening Test is given to all children yearly.

PLAY INTERVIEW

At times a play interview is conducted to observe children in a less-structured situation, particularly if the response to the standard instruments was limited. Such an interview is useful with highly oppositional and extremely withdrawn children, offering a glimpse into their personality.

PSYCHOLOGICAL REPORT

A comprehensive report, combining all the findings, is written. The results of the speech evaluation are not included unless language problems were a referral concern.

THE CHILDREN'S CENTER PSYCHOLOGICAL REPORT

**The Children's Center
Developmental History & Assessment**

                                          TIME:

                                          DURATION:

1.   Identifying Information   DATE 11-5-80

      Name of Child: Jimmy O.   DOB: 10/20/76 Age: 4-0

      Parent(s): Ben and Ann

      Information obtained from: Mother and dad

      Referred by: Mother   Physician: Dr. Blue

      Day Care/School: Snow White

      Describe basic family. Specify marriages, divorces,

      and current living arrangements.

            Ann, 24 - Ben, 28 - Mary, 2 - Betty, 6 mos.

2.   Chief Complaint: (State parent'(s)' global concerns)

            Very poor peer relationships, aggressive

3. Presenting Problems: (Behaviors and duration)
    Aggressive toward peers and siblings, oppositional
    and noncompliant, separation problems past few
    months, unresponsive to discipline.

4. Social History:

    a. Infancy (feeding, sleeping, toileting, talking,
        walking): Poor sleeper, up every few hours,
        walked 10 mos., talking 1½ years, toilet trained
        at 3 - wets at night.

    b. Temperament (global mood, bonding, cuddly) -
        present affective states: High activity level,
        requires lots of attention, not very cuddly.

    c. Present sleeping and eating patterns: Insists
        that parents check on him every 10 minutes until
        he falls asleep, won't sit through whole meal.

    d. Speech and language skills: No problems.

    e. Attention span, impulsivity, activity level,
        favorite toys/activities: Short attention span,
        constant motion - likes cars, Ninja turtles - able
        to only handle one request needs

    f. Large and small muscle coordination: Very well
        coordinated, good small motor.

    g. Self-care skills (dressing, toileting, etc.):
        Dressing O.K., sleeping problems (see 4.a).

    h. Habits/rituals/anxieties (thumbsucking,
        masturbation, nail biting, etc.): Picks nose.

    i. Interactions with parents, siblings, and peers:
        Mother - tough time separating, demands her
        constant attention. Father - limited time
        together. Peers - aggressive if not getting his

own way. <u>Sister</u> - continuous conflict. <u>Baby</u> -
quite helpful, enjoys caretaking.

j.   Significant separations/crises (include
physical/sexual abuse): Vacations - stays with
grandparents, hyper and anxious.

k.   Discipline (agreement between caretakers): Time-
outs, spankings - "It doesn't hurt."

l.   Current performance at day care/school: Attention
problems, high activity - has to be boss and be in
charge.

m.   Like best about child: Tender-hearted, lots of
energy, sense of humor.

n.   List 3 strengths and 3 weaknesses about the child:
Gets along well with adults, good sense of humor,
leadership potential - Poor peer relationships,
sibling conflicts.

o.   Whatever was not asked:

5.   Previous treatment history/medical:

a.   Pregnancy and delivery. (Drug and alcohol use?
Planned?): Stressful delivery, 6 lbs. 1 oz.,
mother developed severe migraines.

b.   Medical problems (medication, allergies, tubes,
seizures, hospitalizations, accidents, head
trauma): Pretty healthy.

c.   Previous mental health counseling. (List any
prior/current therapists or agencies involved.):
Brief consults.

6.   Family psychiatric history (depression, suicide, ADHD,
learning problems, alcohol/drug abuse, schizophrenia):

7. Drug and alcohol use:

    a. List any prescription/over-the-counter meds
        currently using: None.

    b. Drug related reactions/allergies: None.

8. Initial formulations: See Psychological Evaluation
    Summary

    DSM III-R Diagnosis:

    Axis   I.   313.00 Overanxious Disorder

    Axis   II.   None

    Axis   III.   None

    Axis   IV.   2 - (stressors): New position in family

    Axis   V.   Current GAF: 45

                    Highest GAF past year: 45

9. Disposition: Day RX

10. Signature:

11. Supervisor:

Confidential Report

Jimmy O.	TIME: 10:00 DURATION: 2 hours
DOB: 10/20/76	DATE: 11/80
AGE: 4-0	EXAMINER: Licensed Psychologist

Referral Source and Reason

Jimmy was referred to The Children's Center by his mother. Referral concerns included aggression toward peers and siblings, oppositional and noncompliant behaviors, a failure to respond to discipline, and a development of separation problems over the past several months.

Background Information

Jimmy is the oldest child of Ben and Ann. He has two younger siblings—Mary, who is two years old, and Krista, who is one month old.

Jimmy attends Snow White Day Care. Mother reported that his teacher has observed a poor attention span, a high activity level, and poor peer relationships, as Jimmy insists on being in charge of play situations. His parents indicated that he demands constant attention at home. He is in constant motion and requires frequent redirection. Father noted that Jimmy is able to handle only one request at a time. If they make more requests, Jimmy is unable to successfully follow through.

Appearance and Behavioral Observations/Mental Status

Jimmy is an attractive child with blonde hair and blue eyes. He had no difficulty separating from his parents and played quietly in the waiting area while his parents were interviewed. When asked to enter the testing room at the conclusion of the developmental interview, Jimmy shook his head to indicate his refusal. His parents reassured him that it would be alright to go with the examiner, at which point he grudgingly entered. Once inside the office, he immediately said, "I don't like to color!" The examiner assured Jimmy that he would not have to color, at which point he willingly seated himself at the table. Jimmy communicated easily and was able to sustain good eye contact. After the first few minutes, he was more at ease and appeared comfortable in the company of an adult. A relationship was easily established.

During the evaluation, Jimmy demonstrated delight over his successes; however, he was quickly frustrated when he encountered failure. He responded by becoming increasingly oppositional and demanding that the testing session be terminated. He was easily distracted and was in constant motion in his seat. Jimmy was kept on task with frequent prompts and a fast pace of presentation of the test materials.

Tests Administered

Stanford-Binet Intelligent Scale–Fourth Edition
Developmental Test of Visual-Motor Integration (VMI)
Draw-A-Person (DAP); Draw-A-Family (DAF)
Plenk Storytelling Test (PST)
Child Behavior Checklist (CBCL)
Temperament Assessment Battery for Children (TABC)
Connors Parent Questionnaire

Test Results and Interpretations

Jimmy's measured IQ on the Stanford-Binet places him within the high-average range of intelligence and ranks him at the eighty-fourth percentile when compared to his same-aged peers. A significant strength was manifested on the Verbal Reasoning subtest, as his score placed him at the ninety-seventh percentile. He performed below expectancy on the Quantitative Reasoning subtest (45 percent), which likely reflects a lack of motivation and/or exposure to number facts.

Jimmy completed the VMI using his right hand and a firm pincer grip. He easily completed seven of the figures, yielding an age equivalent score of four years, ten months. Visual-motor skills are clearly well developed.

When asked to draw a picture of a person, Jimmy stated, "I'm gonna make a sad person." He drew a large, poorly integrated stick figure with large ears (see Figure 4.1). Jimmy then turned the paper over and said, "Now I'll make a tiger with sharp teeth!" (Figure 4.2). Jimmy's response suggests ambivalent feelings concerning aggression but also indicates anxiety around interpersonal relationships. His family drawing began with a circle and "one eye" for his sister. Two circles on each side depict his parents. They also only have "one eye." The three circles are connected with lines that Jimmy indicated were arms. Jimmy then drew himself below the three figures with large outstretched arms and long legs. The baby is left out of the picture. His drawing suggests anxiety regarding the family system and a tendency to engage in power struggles with his parents, for Jimmy appears to view himself as the most powerful family member.

Jimmy's responses to the PST are unusually brief for a child of his verbal ability. He tends to deny his aggressive impulses, for a picture of two boys fighting was turned into a happy hunting scene. Parental figures are described positively, as are peer relationships. Anxiety was noted in one picture as he created a story about a girl getting run over by a car. The mere thought seemed to increase his anxiety as he quickly decided that it was "just a parking lot" instead. To a picture of a small boy sitting in a boat touching the water, he said:

"He is in a boat . . . touching the water. (*What will happen?*) He'll sink, never get back up . . . there are sharks in there, get eaten. (*Will somebody help him?*) No, there is nobody there."

For the most part, Jimmy attempted to provide socially desirable responses and thus resisted revealing much information about himself.

The CBCL was completed by mother. Her responses place Jimmy above the ninety-eighth percentile in the areas of depression, aggression, and delinquent behaviors. The resulting profile suggests that Jimmy tends to angrily act out his feelings, and his behavior may be masking some underlying depression and anxiety.

Both parents completed the Connors, and their responses yielded scores of 2.0 and 2.4 respectively on the hyperactivity index. These scores place Jimmy well within the range of children who are seen to exhibit severe problems with lack of attention and hyperactivity.

The TABC indicates that Jimmy exhibits a high energy level. He

Figure 4.1
A Sad Person

"I AM GONNA MAKE A SAD PERSON."

Figure 4.2
A Tiger with Sharp Teeth

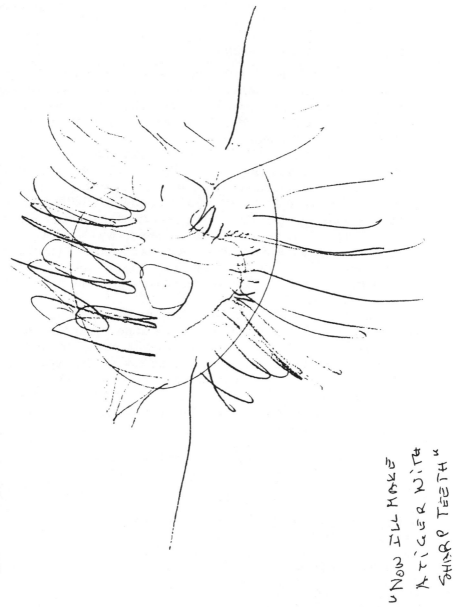

"NOW ILL MAKE A TIGER WITH SHARP TEETH"

tends to adapt well to most situations and warms up to new people with relative ease. He expresses his feelings with a high level of intensity. Jimmy is not easily managed by attempting to distract him and he does little to solve his own problems when he is angry or upset.

Summary and Recommendations

Jimmy is a four-year-old child who was referred to The Children's Center by his mother. Referral concerns included aggression toward peers and siblings, oppositional and noncompliant behaviors, a failure to respond to discipline, and a development of separation problems over the past several months.

The present evaluation finds Jimmy to be a child of high-average intellectual skills and superior verbal skills. Visual-motor abilities are also well developed. Emotionally, Jimmy presents with a high activity level, distractibility, and impulsivity. Much of his irritability is likely to be related to his need to control; however, there is also some indication of underlying feelings of anxiety and sadness to which he may be responding. He easily engages in oppositional behaviors and power struggles at home, for he perceives himself to be the most powerful member of the family. In general, there is some anxiety associated with interpersonal relationships.

It is strongly recommended that Jimmy be admitted to an activity therapy group at The Children's Center. Treatment goals should focus on developing interpersonal relationships with peers and adults, increasing his compliance, and decreasing his anxiety and aggression. A medical consult is also recommended in order to assess his high activity level. It will be essential for his parents to be involved in parent treatment in order to gain the requisite skills for controlling his complex behaviors at home.

Licensed Psychologist

A psychiatric consultation was requested by staff prior to discharge.

THE CHILDREN'S CENTER PSYCHIATRIC CONSULTATION

Confidential Report

NAME: Jimmy O.   DATE: 10/81
DOB: 10/20/76   TIME: 30 minutes
C.A.: 4-10   DURATION: 1 hour (includes write-up)
                   EXAMINER: MD, Child Psychiatrist

Identifying Information

Jimmy is a four-year, ten-month-old boy who lives with his parents and two younger siblings. He has been in day treatment at The Children's Center since December, 1980. This consultation was requested for treatment planning.

Jimmy was originally assessed in November 1980 with referral concerns of his aggression toward peers and at home, noncompliance, separation problems from his mother, demand of adult attention, and high activity levels. The psychological evaluation found Jimmy to be a bright, coordinated child who was preoccupied with aggression and anxious around interpersonal relationships. He was also very active, distractible, and impulsive. On a recent evaluation, he drew a happy self-portrait on the Human Figure Drawing Test. His response to the boy in the boat was as follows:

He touches the water. Ooops, he'll fall in. (*What will happen?*) He can swim, he'll make it. (*Will anybody help him?*) No . . . he can do it.

Treatment Summary

In treatment at The Children's Center, Jimmy has been noted to have high levels of anxiety, appearing tense and nervous, particularly in new settings or situations where he cannot be in control. He would pace the floor, pound his hands together, need to go frequently to the bathroom (with occasional enuresis), and need frequent reassurance from the therapists. He developed a relationship with a peer in which he domineered, but he would also become extremely anxious if the child was unavailable. He would overreact to adult prompts, bursting into tears. He also had high energy levels initially but very quickly settled to routines that demanded concentrating in a structured setting, such as art activities or circle time with stories. He was perfectionistic and became frustrated in projects that did not meet his expectations.

During treatment, Jimmy made improvements in all areas described. He plays interactively with peers without aggression, although he still demonstrates a need to be in control. His activity levels have settled to an average level for his age, and he continues to attend to pre-academics well. He is less frustrated in activities, and therefore his temper outbursts and teasing of peers has diminished. He is more self-confident and seems generally happier and more outgoing (Figure 4.3).

Examination

Jimmy is a very handsome, average-sized, almost five-year-old boy. He separated easily from his group to accompany the examiner, despite having had only a few brief meetings previously. He had excellent

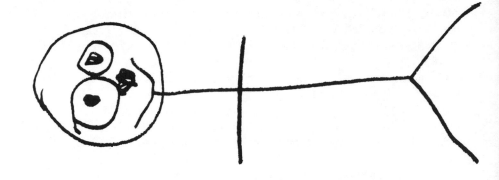

Figure 4.3
A "Happy" Jimmy

language skills and answered questions comfortably. He was interested in activities, attended well to some difficult tasks, and managed his frustration over not being able to build a complicated block structure without it collapsing. After several attempts, he was able to laugh with the examiner over the failures. On several occasions he was distracted from the activity at hand and would wiggle restlessly in his chair, but otherwise he attended well during the thirty-minute session. He spoke positively about his performance in group, stating that he comes to The Center "to learn to get along with kids." When asked how he was doing, he stated, "Really good. I've got friends."

Impression/Recommendations

Jimmy is an almost five-year-old boy who has responded extremely well to nine months of day treatment in a preschool activity group and family therapy. He is much calmer, more focused, and able to relate to peers, function in his home, and enjoy himself without overreacting to frustration. He continues to exhibit very mild symptoms of attention deficit disorder, but overall his initial hyperactivity and distractibility were most likely related to anxiety. He continues to demonstrate a strong need to be in control.

His excellent progress in treatment suggests he will soon be ready for a regular preschool setting. He does best in a more structured setting in which he can receive frequent positive social input for his excellent academic skills and have continued support to help manage his frustration when he becomes overly perfectionistic or bossy.

Reviewing treatment progress and past reports, I feel he suffered from overanxious disorder (313.00), which has now improved dramatically. Discharge to be considered.

Child Psychiatrist

DISPOSITION MEETING

The report is discussed with the parents, and upon their request and with their written permission reports are sent to the referral source.

A complete assessment prior to intervention is crucial and should include standardized testing, observations of behavior, a developmental history, and a play interview. Techniques presented provide a holistic approach for evaluating the troubled child and result in conceptualizing the causes of the child's anxiety or antisocial behavior.

The treatment model at The Children's Center is being used effectively with preschool and young school-age children (Freston, 1991) with different behavioral problems. A flexible and versatile treatment team is needed to help children change their behavior pattern through the use of a variety of intervention techniques.

Chapter 5

The Interdisciplinary Treatment Team

INTRODUCTION

For many years group care of preschool children was limited to preschools for the well-to-do and was neglected by theoreticians as well as practitioners. The reasons for this neglect might well be historical as well as economical. Historically, the family took care of young children's emotional, physical, and cognitive development. Outside influences were only minimally available and frequently disdained. The mother's place was in the home, and she was in charge of the children's upbringing until they entered school. Social interaction was limited to Sunday school or the neighborhood. Major social changes during the late nineteenth and twentieth centuries, due to a large extent to industrialization, did emphasize the need for group care for young children. Though even in those early days, some evidence was forthcoming concerning the importance of early learning, little was done for the population at large.

The cultural lag between scientific findings and practical application of them is tremendous. It took a long time for the people in power to realize that early childhood education, just like later education, must be provided for all children if later dire consequences are to be avoided (Schorr, 1989). Recognizing this need, the federal government in the 1960s began the Head Start Program, providing early stimulation and positive emotional experiences for four-year-olds growing up in poverty. Parental involvement added greatly to the program's success.

Many experts agree that even age four is too late to begin emotional preparedness for school. Public policy strategies are now needed to start program "Heart Start: the emotional foundation of school readiness" (Mitchell-Meadows, 1992), for children between ages zero and three. Certainly children who show maladaptive behavior patterns at ages two and three need to be reached at birth. Delayed language development, poor small-motor coordination, and cognitive handicaps prior to entering kindergarten lead to school failure and subsequent dropout. The emotional handicaps of poor impulse control and low self-esteem, as well as the lack of interpersonal relationships, add substantially to failure. Absence of an attachment to a significant adult caretaker frequently results in antisocial acting out.

With the rapidly increasing number of young children in trouble, treatment facilities are badly needed. Intensive intervention for preschool children has been an even more neglected field than regular preschool and day-care facilities. Some of this neglect might be due to the exclusive use of the medical model in the treatment of emotional problems, totally overlooking environmental factors.

THE INTERDISCIPLINARY TEAM

One of the newer developments in the treatment of mental illness and in the work with emotionally, intellectually, and physically at-risk children is the interdisciplinary intervention team. After mental patients were released from "snake pits" where only custodial care was offered, treatment in mental hospitals was directed by physicians who relied heavily on the nursing staff. When emphasis shifted to more specific diagnosis and outpatient treatment, clinical psychologists entered the field. The discovery was soon made that the total environment plays an essential role in the rehabilitation of mental patients. Enter the social worker.

For quite a long time the pecking order of M.D., Ph.D., and M.S.W. was *the team*. Use of movement therapy on a children's ward created quite a stir in the late 1940s at a well-known midwestern psychiatric clinic. The team expanded to include music and art specialists, special education teachers, and recreational and occupational therapists. Even today none of these nor speech therapists are recognized as "healers" and, therefore, are not reimbursed by insurance companies. Nevertheless, all these players now form the interdisciplinary team used in psychiatric hospitals, in outpatient treatment centers, on pediatric wards, and in some special classroom units to the benefit of patients of all ages and with a variety of diagnoses.

Each professional group contributes the special skills acquired in the training of its members to provide a variety of services needed in the treatment of children with emotional problems. In school systems, specialists can and do fill these roles, helping teachers to provide special services within a more academic environment than mental health clinics.

THE CHILDREN'S CENTER TEAM

In 1963 the original team at The Children's Center consisted of two nursery school teachers and a psychologist-director for a twelve-children facility, which at that time was part of a regular preschool. A social worker was hired almost immediately to work with the parents. As the number of seriously disturbed children increased, a part-time child psychiatrist was added, followed by a speech therapist. Social work and psychology students were accepted as trainees. A movement therapist joined the team next, and recreational therapists worked as child therapists as more groups were established. It was quickly recognized that in milieu therapy the office staff also needed to have special qualities to deal with the families.

Since its inception, the Center has steadily grown and with it the members of each professional group. At the present time The Children's Center has thirty-two half-time child therapists, one full-time and one half-time child psychiatrist, two full-time licensed psychologists, one half-time Ph.D. and four graduate psychology students, six full-time social workers and four graduate social work students, and three consultants in psychiatry, psychology, and social work, respectively. Four group home counselors, one movement specialist, one speech therapist, one full-time and one half-time infant specialist, and a full-time kindergarten outreach coordinator complete the major clinical workforce. A full-time day-care coordinator, plus an assistant, and a part-time social worker comprise the team for educational services. (An annual report is available from The Children's Center.)

The administrative director, a clerical staff of twelve, and six bus drivers and a supervisor comprise the rest of the team. Three hundred and four staff volunteers lend their support to the agency.

The largest number of professionals working at the Center, and in many ways the most important, are the child therapists.

THE ROLE OF THE CHILD THERAPIST

Different theoretical models assign various roles to the therapists in group therapy (Whittaker and Small, 1977). Behavioral models see the adult as a trainer, a reinforcer, a monitor, and a teacher. In dynamically oriented groups, the adult is an active force helping children deal with internal impulses and external demands. More recently, roles have become less specifically defined, leading to more eclectic applications of these theories.

The Children's Center is an example of the changing role of the therapist during different phases of intervention.

Prerequisites

Requirements for the job of a child therapist at The Children's Center are an open mind and positive childhood experiences. Having played as a child or played with one's children, formed a positive attachment to a caregiver, and demonstrated creativity and flexibility—those are essential qualities. Knowing how to play, sitting on the floor, and not being distressed by noise, runny noses, toileting accidents, "bad language," and peculiar eating habits help greatly. A general positive attitude and lively affect are desirable.

Academic prerequisites are a college degree in liberal arts or extensive experience working with children. Of equal importance with academic credentials, however, are personality traits: patience, a good sense of humor, awareness of one's own "hang-ups," and, probably most importantly, a belief in people's ability to change.

Interest in continued learning about human behavior and in developmental and abnormal psychology, as well as involvement in social issues concerning children and families, is helpful. Empathy toward the families and the children not colored by undue sentimentality is essential. Many of the children are waiflike little persons, and the conclusion that "love is enough" is misleading in a therapeutic environment.

The majority of the child therapists are female and Caucasian, though we are continuously on the outlook for minority women and men in general. They, especially men, are hard to find. Our society has not stressed the importance of male figures in the development of young children. At the present time, when so many children are growing up without stable male models, the urgent need for such professionals has increased.

Responsibilities

Each group has a primary therapist and a co-therapist. The primary therapist carries the major responsibility for programming and for supervision of the co-therapist and the volunteers. Most primary therapists have come up through the ranks, initially working at the Center as co-therapists. Prior to being hired, many professionals have worked at the Center as volunteers or students.

Programming for nine children—each at different phases of treatment, in different developmental stages, and with a variety of diagnoses—for a three-hour period daily and for twelve months of the year is a tall order. Hands-on supervision of co-therapists and volunteers demands a basic knowledge of child development, personality dynamics, behavioral techniques, and programming ideas.

The complexity of their role becomes clear after observing the manifold aspects of their job. Tracking the total group with regard to positive and negative interactions of each group member, activities, and ambiance of the room is primary. Group therapy is based on peer interaction under the guidance of the therapist; the "general" needs to know at all times what the troops are doing. Surprises initiated by a group of disturbed children are not therapeutic in most instances. The demands also include ability to write reports, gain from supervision, and tolerate the noise and commotion of a group of small children on a daily basis. Burnout often occurs, and attempts are made to avoid it by continued support and training.

Dealing with these many challenges is extremely demanding. We have found that working in only one group is the limit for most people, particularly if therapy is perceived "as an encounter with a definite purpose" (Bruch, 1974). Demands on the therapist's own emotional stability, flexibility, and sense of humor are great—almost impossible if one brings one's own problems to the job. A support system for the therapist is essential in times of personal crisis.

CO-THERAPISTS

Co-therapists are selected equally carefully. Proper pairing of primary and co-therapists is vital—and often difficult to achieve. If possible, each should balance the other's abilities and share the other's value system. A male-female combination is particularly desirable in the groups of four-and five-year-old children, as they seem to need male models even more urgently than the younger ones. If this cannot be achieved, male volunteers are channeled into these groups. The primary therapist serves as model for the co-therapist; this relationship, in many instances, is a learning experience for both. It is helpful to the group when the therapist remarks to the co-therapist or the volunteer about the children's action or about group activity. For example, the therapist might say, "Mary is almost ready," thereby preventing the adult's help; or he or she might remark, "Everybody is hungry, so let's get snack ready," showing the children that adults can make requests of each other in a positive way.

SUPERVISION AND STAFF TRAINING

Supervision is a tricky area that takes experience and "people skills." It works best if the therapists ask questions, weigh answers, and feel free to discuss issues. Each child's progress relating to treatment goals is discussed, total group constellation is considered, and program suggestions are made. The special rapport that develops between therapist and co-therapist also needs to exist between therapists and supervisor.

Supervision is done by the staff psychiatrists, experienced social workers, and licensed psychologists, and ideas are shared in biweekly sessions of several hours' duration. Supervision encompasses the therapists' verbal reports, frequent visits in each group, observation through the one-way window, and discussion in weekly staff meetings. Clinical reports and anecdotal notes are reviewed and treatment plans brought up to date in these biweekly sessions. Ideally, these are freewheeling discussions rather than didactic sessions.

Training at The Children's Center starts with an orientation for new staff members that includes written material (Plenk, 1978), an article written by a trainee (Ostrom, 1982, see Appendix C), and a reading list (see Appendix D). Weekly staff meetings are conducted by various staff members and outside experts in special areas like neurology, audiology, and legal issues affecting children. Participation in professional workshops in the community and in ongoing research at the Center is encouraged. Some therapists participate in the mother-toddler program and the afterschool groups for children ages five to seven, enabling them to observe developmental stages in younger and older children.

ROLE IN THE GROUP

The therapists must set the group norms in the therapeutic environment. They need to be relaxed without being permissive, structured without being inflexible, fun without being overstimulating, didactic without being stultifying. Such a nonthreatening environment makes self-protective aggression less necessary, lessens anxiety, and replaces aggression with assertiveness. Children learn to express negative feelings, either verbally or through an appropriate activity. This, in time, will lead to selection of socially permissible behaviors.

For many children who have not developed inner controls, lacking appropriate early models and positive relationships, freedom of expression is difficult to handle.

By accepting the child's need to express negative feelings—but not the behavior—the therapists show their nonjudgmental attitude and thus provide a basis for positive relationships. This reduces conflicts and increases the children's confidence in adults and their ability to negotiate. Most young children with behavior problems have failed with adults and need to establish a level of confidence in adults' judgment, fairness, and concern for their well-being. If this does not happen, children will fight the establishment, personified for them in their parents, school systems, and society as a whole. By offering themselves as models and by thoughtful appropriate programming, the therapists provide opportunities for positive achievement and substitutions for missed earlier gratifying experiences. The assumption that reflection will clarify children's negative impulses and that their own "self-actualizing drives" (Axline, 1969) will help in making changes has not proven helpful in a group setting. Prolonged nondirective techniques used in a group setting can lead to the group's total disintegration, since negative behaviors are often contagious and children assume tacit approval by the therapist if no intervention is forthcoming.

Active intervention in group interaction is important. Assume the following scenario.

Johnny cannot get his foot in his boot to go outside. He pitches it across the room and hits Mary. She, in turn, pitches his boot and hers. Total bedlam results. The therapist swiftly moves in and retrieves both boots with the remark, "Boots are for wearing, not for throwing." She then helps each child put them on, saying, "Johnny, maybe you need larger boots. Throwing them will not make them bigger. Let's find you another pair. Mary, you are ready now; let's go outside."

The hope is that the co-therapist and the volunteers have moved the other children out the door. To save the group atmosphere demands swift action, a good sense of humor, and control of nonverbal behavior. The face is the only part of the body that cannot be hidden, and an angry or helpless expression on the therapist's face can ruin the situation. Young children expect solutions and help from adults, and if these are not forthcoming, doubt as to the adult's strength and a lack of trust result. The therapist needs to be aware of the sociometric constellation of the group. Had Johnny's boot hit Craig, a child with even less impulse control but with a leading position in the group, a fight would have ensued, demanding physical intervention.

TRANSFERENCE

Children often attempt to repeat their relationships with parents or a caregiver by putting the therapists into the established mold. It is crucial for the therapists to recognize this transference and not take on the parental roles. By remaining objective but concerned outsiders, therapists facilitate the therapeutic process.

Peter, age 3, finished snack daily but dawdled while eating his lunch. At times he threw it out altogether; other days he lost it on the way from the bus to the Center. Through discussion with Peter's caretaker, it was learned that mealtime, particularly lunch, was a struggle. Peter was urged to eat, even fed when he refused to finish a meal. Handling of these incidents was inconsistent: Father let it go; mother and baby sitter insisted on Peter's finishing his meal. Peter expected the same response from the therapists and was quite baffled when it was not forthcoming.

When the therapists handled his eating matter of factly and did not urge him, he stopped transferring his earlier behavior and began to finish his food. It was at the same time pointed out to him that extra attention was available to him; he had only to ask.

Knowledge of family dynamics was also necessary to handle the following transference situation.

Mary Ann, age 5, was referred for intense struggles with her mother that ended in severe tantrums of long duration. One of the recurrent incidents concerned daily morning hair combing. Mary Ann wore her hair long and was proud of it. She brushed and combed it herself, but mother frequently wanted to do it over, and struggles ensued. When Mary Ann entered treatment, her mother was encouraged to let her do it by herself. When Mary Ann appeared at times with messy hair, she expected therapists to finish the job and was cross when they did not do it. She reacted negatively, expecting the therapists to act like her mother, and started to fight them, even though they did not comb her hair.

COUNTERTRANSFERENCE

The therapists' own background, relationships, and personality are reflected in their handling of the children, and these elements need to be considered in all interactions.

Kristi was quiet and isolated from the other children. After several months in treatment she related well to the therapist, but she still showed no outreach to children. When this was pinpointed during supervision with senior staff, the therapist remarked that she truly understood Kristi's behavior, since she herself was shy in social situations with peers. When she became aware that her own feelings supported Kristi's isolation, she created situations furthering outreach to peers.

SPECIAL STRESS SITUATIONS

Discharge of children or changes into another group evoke strong feelings of loss—and, yes, at times, even grief—in the therapists. Regardless of whether or not the treatment was successful, the therapist experiences a feeling of loss. The satisfaction of having been helpful to the children is recognized at the intellectual level, but the emotional pain is frequently overlooked by co-workers and supervisors.

THE ROLE OF THE SOCIAL WORKER

Parent Therapy

Parent therapy is the major responsibility of the social work staff. They conduct all didactic parenting classes and counsel parents individually, conjointly, or in groups. The involvement of parents in the treatment of their children is essential. This is particularly true when dealing with preschool children because their personality development depends to a great extent on the modeling of, and relationship with, their parents.

The Families

Poverty, violence, increased use of drugs, and disruption of family life through divorce and abandonment have created dysfunctional and disengaged families in larger numbers than ever before. The results of such social ills can be seen in the steadily increasing numbers of young children with severe behavior problems. Lack of adequate housing, resulting in unstable living conditions, affects young children, adding to their sense of insecurity and impermanence.

Preschool-aged children, more than any other group of children, are dependent upon their parents for physical care, emotional support, and guidance. Such support includes modeling of coping skills that will serve them in the world at large, in communication, and in the appropriate handling of affect. The family environment in many cases lacks permanence and is unpredictable and inconsistent, thus depriving children of patterns of experience they can use in problem solving. Frequent changes in caretakers expose children to widely diverse handling of situations without providing them with a stable working model. Parents' inconsistency in responding to their children's behavior results in confusion and a low sense of self, making it impossible for them to use earlier experiences as general guidelines. Rules applied inconsistently cannot be internalized, making children dependent on adult input rather than furthering independent conflict resolutions. Inability to handle situations successfully in turn leads to inappropriate problem solving, resulting in clashes with established patterns outside the home situation. Such negative experiences will make the outside world a dangerous place in which to operate, which then in turn leads either to avoidance of that environment or to violent attacks. Neither solution is satisfactory. The vicious cycle of unsuccessful experiences will become larger and larger, continuing to create problems for the child and the family.

It is at this point that families come to treatment or more likely are referred by the "outside world," which is unable to handle the child. In general, parents do not recognize that their lifestyle as well as society has created or contributed to the existing problem. They appear at an agency with a predominantly child-focused agenda, solely to have the child "fixed." The parents' lack of understanding of their role in the creation and continuation of the problem is one of the major hurdles that the therapist working with the parents has to overcome (Minuchin, 1967).

In many instances, parents of young disturbed children are defensive and angry about their need for help. The need for therapy is looked upon as a sign of failure by the parent and often also by the extended family.

Evaluation of Parents

An initial interview with parents and the completion of a family history are necessary to develop collateral treatment goals (French, 1977). At times, parents see the treatment goal only in terms of the child's behavior, and it is necessary to comply with this request. Too early attempts at pinpointing parental problems can lead to removal of the child from treatment altogether. Establishment of a working alliance between the parent therapist and the parent needs to be based on the parents' confidence and belief in the agency's ability to help them and their child.

Psychological assessment of the children and the taking of a developmental history seem to stress the child as the identified patient. Experience over the years has shown that this emphasis might be misunderstood by parents, leaving them with the impression that they are of less importance in the treatment process. To overcome this fallacy, several attempts have been made to include parental checklists like the Achenbach Behavioral Checklist (1983) and the Parental Stress Index (Abidin, 1986) in the initial evaluation. Use of more specific instruments geared to the parents' own psychological state has been avoided because it might discourage the parents from availing themselves of treatment offered. Such exploration is saved for a later date, when the working alliance between therapist and client has been established.

Family crises that interrupt the treatment process occur with great regularity. The staff must use common sense and understand the family dynamics and community resources available to solve these crises. Prevention of recurrent crises might well be a treatment goal in itself. However, fostering dependency and helplessness in the parent does not promote independence for the primary client—the child.

Parent Counseling

To help parents of children in treatment learn to apply behavioral techniques, they are encouraged to participate in time-limited, structured, didactic classes. They meet weekly for eight weeks, and the methods for behavior change that are discussed correspond to the ones practiced in their child's group. The resulting consistency between home and group environments contributes appreciably to the family's progress. In addition, parental attendance at these sessions convinces the children that their parents are equally involved in the process, somewhat removing the stigma of the children as the identified patients and discouraging children from limit testing. Child care is provided.

Simultaneously with the didactic sessions, the parents are seen several times for completion of a family history. Regular biweekly appointments are scheduled during the child's attendance at the Center.

Parents of disturbed children come for help because the children endanger their marriages, their jobs, and, in many instances, their equilibrium. In only rare cases can they recognize the role their upbringing has played in creation and maintenance of the problem behavior. Often parents come for treatment during a crisis. To establish credibility, it is essential to solve the problem that the parents perceive as the most pressing. A child's night terror might disturb a parent more than the child's lack of speech at age three, even though the latter is more alarming to the clinician. Nevertheless, the clinician focuses on the night terror first to meet the need of the parents and gain their confidence in their problem-solving skill. Behavioral management techniques tailored to the child's symptom and reduced to small steps are particularly helpful as the parents' success in achieving changes raises their self-confidence as parents.

Changes in treatment modality are discussed with the parents, and the concepts of interpretation, natural consequences, and reflection are introduced. The use of interpretation and reflection demands insight into family dynamics. It is at this point, when the originally stated problem has been solved, that the emphasis changes from child to parent and the decision has to be made whether a referral for treatment for the parent is needed. Some non-child-related issues like, for example, the father's alcoholism and the mother's denial, now come to the foreground.

A frequent issue is the parents' response to the child's verbalization of negative feelings. It takes insight to understand that earlier symptoms might have been but a displacement of those feelings and that verbal expression of them is preferable and stressed in the child's treatment. However, it often brings the parents' own feelings or shortcomings to the surface; these then need to be resolved, possibly in long-term individual therapy for the parent. Due to the worker's large active caseload with dysfunctional families, long-term cases need to be referred.

Lack of parental participation in counseling or didactic sessions almost always precludes real changes in the child's behavior. Significant behavior problems in young children often occur in dysfunctional families that are unable to keep regular appointments, and in these instances other modalities must be used. Home visits during the time the children are at home are helpful, for it is at home that modeling of parent-child interactions takes place. Many parents have no experience in how to play with their young children, and hands-on situations are apt to be more easily accepted and tried than verbal instructions.

Discharge from the Center is based on the children's achievement of their treatment goal, not on the parents' progress. Several joint child-parent sessions prior to discharge are necessary to determine whether discharge is realistic. Frequently the child is ready, but the parents need a referral for further treatment. Whatever therapeutic modality the parent therapist uses, detailed notes must be taken not only to satisfy the funding source but also to pass clinical information on to the other team members.

Special Problems

Court-referred cases are notoriously difficult and demand very reality oriented, here-and-now management. Contractual arrangements with the parents as to short-term attendance are helpful. Results must be immediate because unfortunately, the families disappear as soon as the imminent threat of court action is removed.

Parents whose children had been removed to foster homes and are returned offer a special challenge. Participation in parenting classes during the children's absence is frequently sporadic and not meaningful; thus, the children return to essentially the same home situation that had necessitated their earlier removal. Counseling with children and parents under these circumstances is often short lived and disappointing for all concerned.

THE ROLE OF THE PSYCHIATRISTS

The medical model has gained increased importance since the biological nature of mental disease has been substantiated by research. The use of medication and, recently, hospitalization has become fashionable. Though young children are only rarely hospitalized, medicating even three-year-olds (for hyperactivity, for example) is not that unusual any more. With the increase in these forms of treatment, the so-called talking techniques have taken a back seat. Despite much data stressing the importance of a combination of medication and psychotherapy, psychotherapy is frequently not done, probably due to elements of cost and time.

Children with medical conditions are being referred to The Children's Center in much greater numbers, adding to its long waiting list and even changing the character of the agency. Cerebral palsy children with behavior problems, for example, have a difficult time maintaining themselves in a group of aggressive, acting-out children. These children move very quickly, create noise, and, at times, might frighten children with special needs by their inappropriate behavior patterns.

Careful evaluation and diagnosis of children who are referred with undifferentiated behavioral and medical problems are the responsibility of the psychiatric team. They see all children with a possibility of medical involvement, prescribe medication, and continue close supervision. Psychiatrists also supervise child therapists, conduct parenting classes, see parents in psychotherapy, and prescribe medication for them.

Because many of the children and their parents are Medicaid recipients, psychiatrists must sign all reports and billing statements. This necessitates their meeting or observing all these families on a monthly basis. Psychiatrists' participation in intake meetings, staff conferences, and didactic sessions extend the other staff members' knowledge.

The University of Utah Medical School, in a contractual agreement with the Center, sends pediatric and psychiatric interns and residents to The Children's Center. Their assignments and supervision are provided by the psychiatric team.

THE ROLE OF THE PSYCHOLOGISTS

Psychologists play an important role in many aspects of the agency's functioning. They assess all children upon referral, and together with the psychiatrist, determine diagnosis and placement in groups. They are also involved in individual therapy with children and parents, and they participate in the infant program. The clinical director of one of the day centers also serves as liaison with Head Start and the preschool classes for the children with special needs. He frequently represents the agency on radio and television.

A Ph.D. psychologist has just recently been added to the staff as director of research to determine the therapeutic efficacy of The Children's Center's approach. The ultimate goal is the establishment of a database that will be used for treatment planning. It is not simple to initiate a research program in a service-oriented organization, particularly one dependent on community funding. It is hoped that the newly created research arm of the Center will devise a sophisticated and reliable system of evaluation of treatment (Zimet and Farley, 1991, pp. 215–244).

Psychologists are also involved in supervising child therapists, interns and residents in clinical and educational psychology, and individual therapy of children and adults.

SPEECH THERAPISTS

Delayed speech and communication disorders affect a large number of children, many of whom also show behavior problems that are directly related to their speech disorders. Children who cannot make themselves verbally understood often express themselves in a physical way, like pushing and hitting, which leads to social isolation, frustration, open conflict, and finally referral for treatment.

Speech development follows a fixed pattern. At first children learn to listen, then to babble, and then to play with sounds. Children who do not follow this pattern or who stop at this stage are in need of a careful evaluation. Early intervention is essential, and the idea that speech problems "go away by themselves" is a myth. Without professional help, children's speech problems will hinder educational achievements and their social development.

The speech pathologist at the Center evaluates all children on admission and at three-month intervals with an audiology and several speech tests. Findings are included in treatment planning and discussed with the parents. Speech therapy is provided in individual and group sessions.

In our highly verbal society, language is part of the cognitive repertory a child must have to succeed. The preschool years are optimal for correcting deficits. It is important to secure the parents' cooperation by handing out word lists and to warn against special attention being paid to stuttering.

MOVEMENT THERAPISTS

Participation of a movement therapist in the program of a treatment agency has proven to be very helpful to many children. At times it opens up a whole new world to little boys, freeing them from the gender bias that only sissies dance. It provides a new avenue of expression for the nonverbal child. Participation in a movement activity has been, at times, the first sign of change in a child's behavior.

In many ways, psychotherapy is a mysterious process, and different means are needed to reach clients, whether they are children or adults.

Ashley, age 2, was referred by her pediatrician. She did not walk or crawl, though no organic reason could be found despite intensive and excellent medical care. She spent much of her time sitting on the floor and then was carried to her highchair for meals. She was an alert and pretty little girl with blond curly hair and large blue eyes. She lived with her parents and a baby brother, age 12 months.

Developmental steps were normal until age 1. She started to crawl but stopped when her brother and mother came home from the hospital. She continued to eat and sleep well but became sedentary and somewhat more quiet than she had been previously.

After medical diagnostic work did not yield any results and with her brother beginning to walk, on the pediatrician's recommendation the family brought Ashley to the Center. After admission procedures, a treatment plan was developed by the staff and parents.

Carried into the group of 2-year-olds by her father, she looked around with interest at the other children. The other children were astonished by her lack of mobility and surrounded her with toys. She played quietly, smiled at the therapists, and showed discomfort only when the other children went outside. It was mentioned to the children that Ashley was not walking, and they reluctantly left her in the room with a volunteer, who occupied herself with getting material ready for the next activity, pulling out a drum and some tambourines.

The next activity was movement therapy! Ashley did not move, but she swayed with the rhythms and clapped with the children. A change was made in the program, and the movement therapist returned the next day. Crawling was part of the activity, imitating a wiggly snake. Ashley laughed but did not crawl. The following week, she tried to raise herself from her sitting position to participate in the same crawling activity, leaned forward, and awkwardly landed on all fours. At this point it was verbalized to the children that Ashley was trying to crawl, and everybody crawled every day. After another week she joined in and then slowly, with help, took a timid first step. Some progress was made every week. She progressed to a walker and then to walking independently.

Music remained her favorite activity and seemed to stimulate her to give up her isolation. Individual play therapy of many months helped her to play out her feelings about the changed home situation.

The movement therapist needs to be aware of each child's problem, the group dynamics, and the child's level of relaxation. Child therapists and volunteers need to participate in the activity. If they do not, children will observe their lack of involvement and also remain distant.

INDIVIDUAL THERAPISTS

The role of the individual therapist within an essentially group therapy modality is important, but auxiliary. Children are referred for individual play therapy by their group therapists for a variety of reasons.

These might include the child's inability to relate to the therapists, overly aggressive behavior toward peers, problems based on sexual or physical abuse, or confusion due to divorce. Psychologists, social workers, and psychiatrists see children in individual sessions.

Some deeply depressed children need the attention and acceptance of a "special friend" before they can permit themselves to reach out to peers. Attachment and bonding need to be established before changes can take place. Therefore, the individual therapist becomes an important person for the child. Material that cannot be dealt with in the group can be handled in individual sessions. With the great increase in referrals for sex abuse, individual play therapy has assumed an increasingly important role. The children are usually seen twice weekly for thirty minutes during their group time. The individual therapist is not used as a disciplinarian by the group therapists, and no reference is made by them to material brought up in the individual sessions. Close cooperation between all members of the treatment team for each case is essential.

Johnnie, 3 years, 6 months of age, had been placed in custody of the Division of Family Services twice and had been in four foster homes prior to admission to the Center. Though exceedingly bright and charming, he had no impulse control and insisted on immediate gratification. He manipulated peers and volunteers and pushed therapists into rewarding negative behavior with attention, since he was unable to accept praise for positive behavior. Johnnie's behavior improved in the foster home but varied greatly in the group. He not only responded to stimulation in the group but, more often than not, was the instigator of trouble. Prior to his return home, individual therapy was added to the total intervention plan. Noticeable improvement occurred until Johnnie's mother became pregnant. During the nine months of a high-risk pregnancy, Johnnie was in constant panic, fearing desertion. He tested limits imaginatively and needed continuous proof that despite the new arrival, he was acceptable and would remain at home. He refused to come to the Center for his group sessions but continued in individual therapy. He was successfully enrolled in a Head Start Program when the family left to join the stepfather in the service. We still hear from Johnnie and his mother, and though he is doing quite well in school, he has problems at home and is in treatment again at a community health center. Continued individual therapy was recommended. (Plenk, 1978, p. 214)

Staff members providing educational services outside of the agency are the day-care consultant, the kindergarten outreach coordinator, and a parent counselor.

AUXILIARY TEAM MEMBERS

Everybody in the building, including clerical staff, is part of milieu therapy. The receptionists often bear the brunt of outbursts by distraught parents. The phones ring incessantly, clinical staff members are in and out, filing piles up, and children create havoc in the waiting area.

Bus drivers are part of our community representatives. Parents and neighbors most often observe their handling of the children. Performing a most difficult, responsible job, bus drivers need and deserve praise and positive input from the clinical staff. They meet monthly with the community outreach coordinator.

Chapter 6
Phases of Treatment

INTRODUCTION

The eclectic nature of treatment modalities used at The Children's Center becomes clear as treatment is carried out according to specific phases.

Phase One can be described as introductory: What is the child doing? What patterns of behaviors used earlier is the child trying out in a new environment? How is the new environment responding? What changes are needed, and how can they be achieved most quickly and successfully leading to the next step? Trust in the therapists, in their consistency and fairness, is essential. Stability of the environment must be maintained. Behavior modification strategies are used.

Phase Two is the greatest challenge for the therapist and the child. The behavioral changes achieved in Phase One will have to be generalized and the question, "Why was the child behaving this way?" answered. New alternate behaviors are introduced through a variety of techniques, with the therapist serving as an auxiliary ego until the children are able to strengthen their own, overcoming denial and resistance to change. Progress will be possible only if a therapeutic alliance is forged between therapist and child. The therapists serve as identification models and are of ultimate importance.

Phase Three revolves around the child's ability to utilize the newly acquired behaviors in social interaction with peers and adults. Dependency on the therapists diminishes, and the child's age-appropriate ego is able to handle problem resolutions on its own. Preparation for discharge concludes this phase.

PHASE ONE OF THE TREATMENT PROCESS

All children admitted to treatment, regardless of diagnosis and chronological age, enter Phase One, which employs behavioral strategies to promote initial changes. Treatment plans have been developed based on psychological assessment, developmental history, reasons for referral, and parental requests.

Since treatment groups are open-ended, whenever one child is discharged, a new one is admitted. Some children are in an early stage of Phase One, whereas others might be ready to move into Phase Two but remain in the same group. Attempts are made to introduce new children into the group at paced intervals. Due to long waiting lists and emergencies, this is not always possible, however.

Some general statements about the children, the therapists, the group atmosphere, the programming, and the interventions in the first phase of treatment follow.

The Children

All the children lack social skills and have fixated on specific behaviors, resulting in maladaptive responses. They have trouble relating to peers and adults and are unable to manage intense affect, which invariably and in short order leads to trouble. They cannot share, wait, or listen; and they do not know how to play. They are overwhelmed by the toys they see and wonder whether the same toys will be here tomorrow. Their need for immediate gratification pushes them to grab, to hoard, and to refuse to take turns. None of their earlier experiences has prepared them for the therapeutic setting: Some of them respond aggressively, while others withdraw anxiously.

The Overly Aggressive Child

The child most frequently referred for treatment is the overly active, aggressive, impulsive youngster who has proved hard to handle in the family and in larger social systems. Running down the aisle in church, intolerable disruptiveness within the family, and inability to listen to a story are seen as danger signals for later school adjustment and lead to referrals.

Lacking basic security, the child expects over and over again to be ignored, cheated, or overlooked, which leads to negative behavior patterns that are usually directed outwardly. Children become angry, fight the outside world, and commit antisocial acts. Their method of dealing with the world is based on their perception that they are not getting their share of goodies and that they are being taken advantage of.

Therefore, they will bully their way to the top. Their fear of losing power pushes them into a panic often expressed in hyperactivity.

The most frequently seen behaviors are physical aggression toward peers, destruction of materials, and verbal insults. These acting-out children become the bane of existence of day-care workers, teachers, and therapists. To calm them takes an excessive amount of time and results in giving attention for negative behaviors, thereby increasing the problem. By the end of their preschool life, these children have already been kicked out of numerous day-care centers and preschools and have been rejected by many teachers.

Mark, age 4, was referred by his day-care center for excessive, prolonged tantrums and had been threatened with expulsion. Antecedents and frequency were not reported. During admission testing the referral behavior was not observed, indicating that in a novel one-to-one situation, even under stress, the behavior was not occurring. The first week in group, Mark participated minimally and spent most of the time observing the children and therapists. On the first day of the second week, when the children lined up to go outside, he became furious when he found out that it was not his turn to be the leader. He threw himself on the floor, knocked over the child taking that position, and screamed obscenities. Immediate intervention was necessary, and Mark was removed to the quiet room. He was observed through a one-way window, and after a few minutes, when he had calmed down, the therapist entered the room. Both then went outside and joined the children. Mark had to wait for a trike but was able to do so while playing ball with the therapist and one of the other boys. When his turn came, he silently rode the trike. The next day he kicked a child next to the therapist off a chair and was again removed from the room. His behavior the rest of the day was subdued. The third day after the first incident, it was his turn to be first in line to go outside, and no incident occurred. All the children lined up well, and each was given a sticker with the remark, "This is a good way to get ready to go out." Mark's tantrums did not occur any more in the treatment group, but they persisted in the day-care center. After three weeks of being placed in time-out, his tantrums diminished to two per week at the day-care center. (See Phase Two for continuation of case report.)

Overactive and aggressive behavior does not always mean that the child is angry. Anxious and depressed children, in their efforts to keep everything moving to cover up their panic, frequently give the same appearance as hyperactive children. However, regardless of the diagnosis, permitting aggressive acts does not help these children but, on the contrary, increases their anxiety.

Peter, age 3, was referred to the Center with a diagnosis of hyperactivity. He was a little wild man in the waiting room and had a difficult time settling down during the assessment. He was distractible, avoided eye contact, and repeatedly said, "I can't do it," during administration of the cognitive instruments. Projective tests indicated Peter's anxiety and lack of trust.

Distractibility diminished with the help of social reinforcement for remaining at an activity, but major progress was made only after he had developed a relationship with one of the therapists.

The Withdrawn Child

Quiet, withdrawn children are much less frequently referred for treatment. If no intervention is forthcoming, they disappear into the woodwork only to emerge as "immature" in kindergarten and then graduate to the "slow learner" group in the early grades. Intellectual deficits rather than emotional factors are often inaccurately assumed to be the reason for the nonfunctioning.

Withdrawn children shun peers, show little interest or initiative in activities, and generally look unhappy. Girls are in greater danger of falling into this category because the "little lady" is still at a premium in our society.

Guidelines for helping anxious, depressed, and withdrawn children during the first phase of treatment encompass more sophisticated techniques than just a simple reward system. These children need plenty of space: Physical and emotional proximity should be avoided (see Figure 6.1). Emotional space means allowing the child time for changes, that is, time to relate to the therapist and to the children, to let go of inappropriate behavior patterns. Physical space means a chair of one's own, an uncrowded place to sit, a place in line, a spot at the easel. Sometimes this idea of space is very difficult for children to comprehend: Their mistrust is so deep and their feeling of trust so fragile that therapists cannot penetrate their defenses.

Nonthreatening material such as easel paint or even water colors can be used rather than finger paints, magic markers rather than crayons. Magic markers are prettier and softer and demand less firmness of touch. Anxious children draw lightly; they are afraid to make a statement! Routine and developmentally correct expectations can be provided, but urging should be avoided, and the therapist needs to remain low-key if the child does not participate. When a child is urged to participate, he is given individual attention, which means reward for unacceptable behavior. Peers can be used to initiate contact, an approach that is much less threatening than input from an adult—and also more novel. Adults need to look for the smallest sign of outreach, like a car being rolled across the table to the therapist, as an entrance into the child's "closed corral" and to reward it nonverbally with participation and a smile. These techniques can be mentioned to the volunteers, who are frequently attracted to withdrawn children and overwhelm them

Figure 6.1
A Space of His Own

Source: Reprinted with special permission of North America Syndicate.

with attention that is contraindicated. A remark to the co-therapist expressing the hope and the optimism that the child will enter the activity that the other children are enjoying is helpful. The basis of the child's seemingly withdrawn behavior—negativism, anxiety, low cognitive skills, depression, low self-concept, fear of risking, inability to relate, learned passive-aggressive behavior, or a need to control—needs to be explored. To find "rewardable" behavior in these children takes more careful observation than with the acting-out child.

The Therapists

The role of the therapists during this phase is extremely demanding. They have to oversee the total group and be aware of every child's action. Their emotional and physical input is intense, and demands on their own strengths are great. They need to be involved, ready to reach out helpfully to the timid, to protect the anxious, and to set limits to stop the aggressor. The activities have to be presented spontaneously, and facial expression and voice need to show interest and involvement. Emotional distance or flatness of affect is counterproductive.

My first experience with the contagion of acting-out behavior occurred in a group of six six- to nine-year-old children who were inpatients in the children's ward at Cook County Hospital in Chicago. The playroom, located on the fifth floor, had no telephone, and there were no other rooms. On a cold and snowy Chicago morning when going outside was not possible, the children decided they wanted hot chocolate—not an unreasonable request. What to do? The children could not be left alone: Edith was psychotic, wandering around the room picking imaginary flowers; Johnny, the newest member, had no impulse control and was anxious to establish himself in the group; Zach had been on the ward the longest and was going home in a week; Mary was hyperactive; and Peter and Jack had been in a number of foster homes and distrusted everybody, asserting that no chocolate would come. The student assigned to the group did not show up that day. The bad weather had an influence on the children and on me. The atmosphere was already unsettled when the hot chocolate issue came up. It was decided after much discussion to send Zach to the fourth floor to get the secretary to call the kitchen to bring us a pitcher of hot chocolate. He departed and did not return. We painted a picture, meanwhile, and then I brought out the clay, which turned out to be a *major mistake.* Johnny got the idea to make a ball out of his and threw it across the room, which started general mayhem. Just before it took on catastrophic dimensions, Zach reappeared with a staff person, a pitcher of hot chocolate, and cookies. Saved by the bell! A good lesson for a new therapist: Don't ever, ever be alone with a group of disturbed children without a phone, and always have a Plan B ready—preferably food.

The Atmosphere in the Group

During this phase, the atmosphere in the group is unsettled. The new children's short attention spans create confusion. They test limits with repetition of earlier inappropriate behaviors that create conflicts. This reminds some of the more settled children of their own problems and makes them uneasy. They watch what is happening with intense interest, observing the therapist's actions and, in many cases, ready to join the fracas. Skillful use of the program can avoid many a calamity.

Frequently, in the first phase none of the referral problems are noted. This stage, labeled by most therapists as "the honeymoon," rapidly evaporates, making room for the "real" little person to appear. Actually, the appearance of the symptoms indicates progress in that the child has become comfortable enough to experiment with acceptance of his true self in the therapeutic environment. This is the first step in the development of trust. A prolonged honeymoon might, at times, indicate that the child's problems are specifically conditioned by a home or school situation.

The Program

The program needs to be structured and consistent from day to day. Activities must promise success experiences; they must be simple and achievable on each child's developmental level, and they must be well planned to avoid chaos. Transitions are hard for children to handle. Cleaning up is a chore to be avoided at all costs. It brings with it much baggage from home, most of it unpleasant, having led to conflict and punishment. Thinking ahead by the therapists and volunteers can avoid confusion and confrontation. It is helpful to start the next activity while one of the children is still picking up; interest in the new activity speeds up the process. Tiredness and being "overworked" need to be recognized as manipulative declarations. It is up to the therapists to set up play situations like grocery stores or trains, for children preoccupied with their problems are not creative. Structured play, play dough, simple puzzles, and short periods of free play are helpful, as is music. Outside time, regardless of the weather, is essential because many children need to release pent-up energy. Cooking is also a good activity at this stage, and eating an even better one.

Interventions

Behavioral Techniques

Experience has proven that behavioral intervention is the most economical way to change these maladaptive behavior patterns. There are a few ground rules for using behavioral intervention strategies: Carefully observe the behavior to be changed, what triggers the behavior—referred to as antecedents—and how often it occurs in a specific time frame (frequency). These facts are necessary to plan behavioral intervention and to measure success or failure. The use of specific strategies depends on the therapist's training and philosophy. Positive reinforcement, rather than the use of cattle prods and other negative means, is preferred by most professionals for legal as well as humanistic reasons. Behaviorists do not look at the reason for a behavior but consider only what they can see (Skinner, 1974).

Nonverbal techniques are most successful at this stage, as many children respond negatively to verbalizations. They expect to be scolded or addressed with short commands like "Pass the bread," "Shut the door," or "Stop kicking sister," and they automatically turn the adult's voice off. Listening to words other than those expressing immediate needs is, for many, a brand new experience.

Requests coming from an adult are often rejected. However, if the request is not directed at them alone, but also at a peer, or if it is phrased with "we," confrontations can be avoided and compliance is achieved. For example, we can ask an "old timer" to help a newcomer come in from the playground, to show him or her how to line up by the door and walk in. This action diffuses the direct request, makes "giving in" less of an issue, and increases the self-esteem of the "old timer." If this approach works, the therapist can praise both children; if it does not, the best response is to reflect optimistically that it will work another day.

Primary Reinforcers

Children who seek immediate gratification respond well to primary reinforcers for positive behaviors. These can be simple finger foods like raisins or pretzels, or more sophisticated rewards like stickers. Whatever their type, reinforcers need to be immediate, given in response to clearly defined behaviors, and used judiciously. In the early stages of treatment, therapists might have to try several times daily to find positive behaviors to reward. The hope is that every child will do something "good" in the course of a three-hour session. The aim of the reward system is to increase positive behaviors, which in time will reduce the negative ones. Primary reinforcers are used when relationships are not yet meaningful to the children.

Primary reinforcers work equally well with aggressive and withdrawn children. The latter group might initially reject them, seeing a raisin as intrusion into their strenuously maintained isolation. Acceptance of a primary reinforcer is, at times, the first indication of a change from earlier behaviors.

Social reinforcers are praise, a hug, a pat on the back, the use of ourselves rather than a sticker. It is a sign of our self-esteem and belief in our influence on the child's behavior. Care must be taken not to automatically say, "Good job," but to try to vary one's remarks, like "This is great," "Look what you can do," "What fun," or "You really did well." Pairing of a primary and a social reinforcer is most effective. A raisin plus a smile doubles the effect.

Intrinsic reinforcers are the enjoyment and the good feeling created by a positive experience even if nobody notices or remarks about it. It is an internal, sophisticated reinforcer reserved for mature adults.

Intermittent reinforcers are used effectively by the inventors of the slot machine. A handful of quarters every fifth pull will keep many people's expectation levels high; thus, they will continue to gamble. The same methods can be used in changing behavior patterns, like reinforcing progress in a child's attending skills—not every time, but on and off.

Time-out has become very fashionable and appears simple to implement; in reality, it is quite complicated. It demands careful observation of the behavior and the antecedents, as well as an immediate response by the adult. Time-out is warranted when the child or the other children are in physical danger, or when the child is overstimulated and needs "quieting." The person removing the child should not show annoyance, anger, or hurt. It is essential to explain to the child the inappropriate behavior that will lead to removal.

Time spent in the time-out room, better called "the quiet room," must be short; and if possible, children should be observed through a one-way window and returned to the group as soon as they are calm. Holding the door from the outside only increases the child's frustration and should not be done. Some children become hysterical, kicking the door, urinating, or screaming. This is not therapeutic, and the adult needs to enter the quiet room and calmly reassure the child. This response transmits acceptance and will calm the child. It is not helpful to discuss the "crime" and even less so to make a moral issue of it. Sometimes tying a shoe, wiping tears, or combing hair helps. When the child is returned to the room, he or she must be aided in reintegrating into the activity. Time-out does not teach new behaviors; at best, it stops old ones.

Removing a child to a chair away from the group (e.g., for tearing up a child's art work) serves a similar purpose as time-out but appears less punitive. The therapist can say to the co-therapist, "Johnny needs to sit out for a minute to calm down, and then he can work on his picture again." The hope is that the child will become interested in the activity and join in. A primary reinforcer is not indicated, but a smile might be nice.

Negative reinforcement like time-out is used only rarely in the early part of the first phase, as it might remind the child of earlier aversive measures. Actions that endanger other children or adults, like throwing chairs or large blocks and making open, unprovoked attacks on children, must lead to removal of the child from the group. However, a better method is prevention of these actions by alert therapists.

Contracting for specific behavior changes is at times effective, but care must be taken that the behavior generalizes rather than stops when the rewards are gone. It is a helpful technique for acting-out, deprived children. They are used to "deals" and may respond favorably. Contracting also helps the child to actually focus on one specific behavior. It is not unusual for a child to remark upon leaving, "I did not hit today," if that was the child's contract. The idea is to establish a positive pattern and then reinforce it with a primary and/or a social reinforcer.

Additional Strategies

Cognitive Reasoning

In our verbal society, cognitive reasoning is often deemed a good way to achieve changes in children's unacceptable behavior; however, reasoning, lecturing, explaining, and reminding do not appear to be effective with young traumatized children. Abuse and neglect in early childhood lead to a limited repertory of emotional expression, to sadness or to rage, to lethargy or hyperactivity. Many children in this group, more and more of whom are crowding treatment centers, rightfully distrust adults and do not see them as helpful or caring. Verbal reassurances per se will not be successful under these circumstances but will be considered as "too little, too late."

Particularly if projected from across the room, an adult voice might go by the children like a breeze; some children are already used to this method and have developed selective deafness and established coping mechanisms. Another danger is that the children will become so used to the adult's decision-making verbal input that it will delay their conscience development. Cognitive intervention can be helpful if it is used in conjunction with the development of problem-solving skills and the teaching of alternative behaviors (Phase Two and Phase Three).

Another useful strategy, when thoughtfully used, is imitation or modeling. Children will model group members as well as therapists and teachers. This necessitates careful grouping as well as awareness on the part of the adults. For an adult to throw a paper cup across the room into the wastebasket is not good modeling for the children, even if the cup hits the basket. Part of the impact of treatment depends on the child's wish to identify with the teacher or therapist: The child smiles when the adult does, observes adults taking turns, and shows prejudice when the teacher or therapist does.

Natural Consequences

The need for direct intervention by an adult and the use of behavioral techniques should diminish after some time in the group. Once the children's observable behaviors have changed and they are convinced of the adult's consistency and fairness, they should be able to accept the use of natural consequences, which are very effective with young children. Natural consequences teach personal responsibility in an impersonal way, are reality oriented, and are cognitively based. Consequences are not punitive, but logical. The child's behavior, not the adult's intervention, leads to the consequence. Not coming in from the playground might lead to missing snack; not listening to a warning about running, to a spill. Children realize consequences and learn from them much quicker if adults avoid moralizing and an "I told you so" attitude. Using this method too early in the treatment process, particularly with abused and neglected children who think that the "world is out to get" them, is contraindicated. Such children will take the consequence as proof for what experience has taught them and then blame the adult, who comes to represent that bad outside world. Differentiating between "good" and "bad" adults needs to be learned.

To Summarize

The major goal of the first phase of treatment is behavioral change, which is achieved by behavioral techniques like positive reinforcement, contracting, and protection from overstimulating situations by removal from the group. These techniques are used because of their immediacy and the symptom relief offered. Developing trust in the environment, experiencing its consistency, coming to understand the strength of the therapists, and having success experiences are major determinants of behavioral change.

No intervention will work immediately. After all, the symptoms, maintained for some time, have afforded the children positive payoff, like special attention—even if it was punishment. Children will try out the same patterns, but through the therapists' interventions, those more socially acceptable will be learned. Replacement of observable behavior is an achievement, but not enough for lasting change.

PHASE TWO OF THE TREATMENT PROCESS

Transition from Phase One to Phase Two, which uses communication to form a therapeutic alliance, is gradual and different for every child. Progression from a reward system (Phase One) to the development of positive relationships and communication depends on a variety of conditions: the severity of the child's disturbance, the group's composition, the family's functioning, and the effectiveness of the therapist. Emphasis is put on communication and the formation of a therapeutic alliance based on this communication. Communication beyond "need" language is extremely difficult for children to learn. It is a brand new experience for them and sometimes also for the therapist, and it requires practice that is gained in this treatment phase.

The Children

Differences between the children referred for aggressive or withdrawn behaviors are now less noticeable. They have both moved toward the middle, learning from each other. The aggressors have discovered new ways to express their needs, as they are now assured of getting their share, at least in the therapeutic environment of the group. On some occasions they still "lose it," but these are rarer and usually can be handled with verbal interventions. The anxious and withdrawn children have realized that being angry is alright, and though still hesitant, they form friendships with the aggressors as if they cherish their ability to act.

Though earlier maladaptive behaviors have often led to rejection, isolation, and even physical harm, giving them up is difficult. Resistance to change is minimized in younger children, particularly within the framework of an activity play group—two realities that have led to the development of The Children's Center's treatment model. Many common forms of resistance in the treatment of children, as mentioned by R. Gardner (1979, p. 415), are avoided by using a peer group and activities as agents of change under the guidance of a trained therapist. Activity group therapy provides a milieu that is very different from anything the child has previously experienced, facilitating the forming of a positive relationship with an adult who can be seen in time as an ally and a helper rather than as an antagonist. The ever-presence of peers during interactions not only provides an experimental field to try out new behaviors but also serves as a control for the therapist's consistency and fairness in a variety of situations.

Schedules are important to many children who come from dysfunctional families. Such children feel threatened by changes in routine and remember instances in their own lives when changes led to abandonment, hunger, and discomfort. Their worry is totally justified, their anxiety increases, and defensive behavior patterns appear.

Johnny, 4 years, 6 months of age, was referred by his day-care center for lack of participation, frequent crying spells, isolated play behavior, and tuning out. Assessment revealed a child with an average I.Q.; good small-motor ability, but a lack of trust in the world around him. Family history established that this was totally based on reality, as the child's mother had left the family rather abruptly and the single father was struggling to manage this child and a younger one without much of a support system and with a full-time job.

Change was slow in coming. For some time, Johnny cried, tuned out, and spent most of his time at the water table with a girl of the same age who was much smaller than he was. The first sign of a breakthrough came when he challenged the therapist about not going outside on a snowy morning: "But you said we always go outside. Now you won't let us." What he really was saying was, "How can I trust you to be here all the time if a little snow makes you change your mind?" The therapist recognized the hidden message and voiced his doubts to Johnny. Although he could not acknowledge that she was right, his behavior changed from that day on. He began to show interest in the other children, developed a nice sense of humor, and used his abilities appropriately. Counseling with his father, which was going on simultaneously, was of great help.

Sometimes the observable behavior is only the cry for help, not the real problem.
Let us now return to Mark.

Mark was originally referred for reacting with excessive tantrums to adult control. His observable behavior in group had greatly improved. Tantrums had ceased. He was making friends in the group, getting along well, and beginning to relate to the therapists. It was still difficult for him to verbally communicate his needs when they conflicted with those of the other children. Behavior at home and in daycare had somewhat improved, but he still made every effort to get his way, though in a less controlling manner.

With Mark, the time had come to use other behavioral interventions in a more systematic way, particularly stressing communication, as he seemed to consider the environment safe and the therapists as friends. Then he went on a short vacation.

When Mark returned, his behavior had regressed. The first tantrum in group occurred the second day following his return. The therapist removed Mark from the room. Rather than taking him to the quiet room, the therapist sat with him in the hall, and the following conversation ensued.

Therapist: You were screaming in line.

Mark: I never get to be first. You don't like me.

Therapist: You think I don't like you because you were not first?

Mark: I was always first on vacation.

Therapist: How come?

Mark: I like to be first.

Therapist: Did you fight about it?

Mark: Yes, but my mom said to let me be first 'cause I am little.

Therapist: Are you little here?

Mark: No.

Therapist: Things here are different. We take turns. I think you can. You did before you went on vacation.

Mark: I'll try.
Therapist: Okay. We'll work on it.

Several more discussions ensued, with examples from home and daycare. The learned behaviors had not sufficiently generalized, and greater inclusion of the family system seemed to be needed.

The other group members are major players during this phase. Each child sees what is going on, hears what is said, and observes the consequences. Subgrouping should begin, supported by interactive play and joint ventures, often during outside play time. Some children whose verbal skills are lagging try new skills on the playground and then transfer them inside with the help of other peers functioning similarly. Cooperative play lasts longer and involves more children. Choices of play material become more varied. Peers provide reinforcement and thus strengthen the child's newfound behavior repertory.

The Therapists

Even though the children have made behavioral changes and the use of behavioral interventions has greatly diminished, the therapist needs to recognize that "rather than introspect, the child tends to act. Rather than view himself as being a contributor to his difficulties, he prefers to externalize and view his problems as caused by forces in his environment" (Gardner, 1979, p. 415). Verbal communication needs to be clear and to leave no room for misunderstandings; requests and directions must be given in positive language. A positive remark delivered in a negative or hesitant tone will come across as negative, particularly to young children who only partially listen but are acutely aware of facial expressions and body movements. Consistency in tone of voice, posture, and facial expression is a must. A child cannot be expected to listen if the therapist shouts from across the room or says something while doing something else. Eye contact must be maintained during conversation. It is best to deal with one child at a time, to make a child wait for a comment rather than to hold one and speak to another.

"With body language, you can reassure, convey security, nurture, redirect classroom movements, motivate, intervene in a developing crisis, decrease discomfort, reward, accept and praise" (Bolster and Wood, 1975, p. 105).

Children are more physically aware than adults. Often, teachers and therapists are oblivious of the speed with which they are moving, the strength of their grip, or the decibel of their voices.

Communication is the cohort of the therapeutic alliance—one is not possible without the other. A secure attachment formed by the child with the therapist is the precursor of both. Once this is established, intervention techniques based on communication and a relationship can be used effectively.

Obstacles to progress may appear. For example, the therapist may become too involved with a child. Too much positive or negative involvement hinders treatment. The therapist may become overly attached to children, depriving them of the opportunity to develop autonomy and emotional independence. The child likes the therapist so much that negative feelings are not brought out at all and, therefore, cannot be worked through. Or the therapist can develop negative feelings toward a child, particularly if progress is lacking despite the therapist's best efforts. These feelings can be expressed in a variety of ways: by overlooking the child and his or her actions, overemphasizing negative behaviors, making concessions, or becoming emotionally overinvolved to compensate, none of which leads to progress in treatment.

An experienced and intuitive supervisor will, in the weekly supervisory sessions, realize what is happening and in an individual session try to be helpful. Because therapists as well as volunteers bring their own family dynamics to work with them, different children will naturally elicit different responses.

To the therapist's consternation, a child may "reach a plateau." It might well be the child's last stand against change or a reflection of home problems. This situation necessitates case conferences with all professionals involved. Solutions might be found in a variety of ways: transfer to another group, addition of another treatment modality such as individual therapy, input from parent therapists, or new ideas for management. Increased understanding of the problems involved and support for the child therapist by the supervisor will result.

The Atmosphere in the Group

The atmosphere is calmer; less limit setting is needed. The children play cooperatively and in groups. Transitions and cleanup have become routine. When a child is unwilling to participate in cleanup, the group discusses consequences. Subgrouping takes place. Outside play is less competitive and makes room for games rather than solitary rides on trikes. The children seem more willing to try out new ideas and behaviors during outside play and then to experiment with bringing them inside.

The Program

The children's attention span has lengthened, and they are now able to become involved in projects like murals or cooking. If a project is not finished by the time the day is done, they can wait to take it home the next day. Taking turns has become easier. Stories can be longer and more complex, and experiences of their own are added to them. Feelings are a topic for group discussion. Individual children are beginning to show interest in their deficiencies in specific areas, like small-motor coordination, and show greater patience in working on them.

We all experience days when children cannot listen to a story. Maybe the story is too long, the pictures not bright enough, the voice too monotonous—or it has already been a hectic day. One child leaves the group and starts running around. Two more join, and the activity is lost. It is best to close the book, telling the children why, and start a movement activity such as galloping in place, singing the "bus song," or doing simple floor exercises combined with primary reinforcers for the children listening. While doing this new activity, it is important to verbalize that the story will be finished tomorrow. The therapist should not take this as a personal affront but might wish to rethink the program of the day, the composition of the group, and the book or activity selected. Children's inability to listen to stories or generally to pay attention is one indication of their anxiety level and should be considered when picking stories or sedentary activities.

Interventions

Social reinforcement is taking the place of primary reinforcers. Removal from the group for unacceptable behavior is less frequent. Verbal intervention techniques, based on therapeutic alliances between the children and the therapists, are the major tools used during this phase of treatment. Communication proceeds on several levels.

Reflecting or verbally rephrasing actions and feelings is an important therapeutic tool. It translates positive as well as negative interactions into words, thus forming a bridge between acting and talking. By reflecting positive as well as negative interactions, the therapists indicate awareness without judgment.

Anni, 3 years, 6 months of age, was a very quiet, somewhat sullen little girl. On arrival she usually threw her jacket on the floor without a word. One day she entered the playroom and hung up her jacket with a cheery hello. Several of the children responded in the same way, and the therapist said, "You are feeling happy today, Anni. I am glad." Pleasure in the group's acceptance and the therapist's acknowledgment of the change will lead to the child's verbal acknowledgment of feelings.

Reflection and/or rephrasing does not demand a response from the child. "When in doubt, reflect" is a good introduction to verbal interventions for both child and therapist.

Interpretations

The next level of communication focuses on interpretation of behavior. Interpretations are statements that attempt to clarify underlying reasons for behaviors. They represent insights gained by the therapists through understanding of the children's environment, the family dynamics, and the children's behavioral repertory. Most disturbed children see their behavior in absolute terms, as good or bad, without a gray area. They need help in understanding, through a variety of techniques, that sometimes one behavior is adequate while at other times it is not. This is a difficult concept to understand at the preschool level and needs continuous repetition in different forms to be useful to the children in generalizing behaviors.

Children might look upon interpretations as pinpointing "badness," and therefore they resist them. They also might be frightened by them, so their use demands great skill on the part of the therapist. Interpretations have to be used thoughtfully, and their introduction as a therapeutic modality depends on a working relationship between the child and the therapist.

F. Pine (1985) differentiates between interpretive and emphatic statements. When two items in a child's life are linked, for example, "You hit because you are feeling angry," intellectual understanding results. The same statement can also be linked to features of the child's life. Mike and Ryan played cooperatively prior to going home, pushing cars along a road. Suddenly Mike hit Ryan. The therapist said, "I think you hit Ryan because you are anxious about your father picking you up, not because Ryan put his car in your garage." Or to a child avoiding cleanup, "It seems to me you are having trouble picking up; I wonder what happens at home." To use interpretations meaningfully, the therapist has to be aware of the specific dynamics of each case and the family circumstances.

In contrast, an emphatic statement, "You are happy," does not link two items together in order to explain an occurrence. It solely promotes self-acceptance and a feeling of acceptance by the other (the therapist). "As the interpretation promotes understanding, the emphatic statement promotes a feeling of being understood" (Pine, 1985, p. 168). At times, labeling a feeling clarifies an inner state. With the help of explanatory statements, the child feels accepted, and acceptance, in time, helps forge the therapeutic relationship. A feeling of acceptance is achieved by the naming of an emotional state; this serves to control or to delay a reaction, neutralizing it for a split second, thus possibly permitting a new solution to be tried.

With young children, emphatic statements have to be based on actions, since the children are not able to express feelings verbally. The therapist clarifies the action by labeling it for the child; labeling does not sanction the action but legitimatizes it and gives the therapist the opportunity to suggest or model alternative behavior patterns.

Interpreting the reason behind a specific behavior may benefit the child, but interpretation can only be done after a relationship has been established. Interpretations should be offered tentatively and introduced with "I think..." or "It seems to me..." rather than the direct confrontation, "You are...." The latter can be too easily denied and then leads nowhere. Interpretation needs to be practiced until the therapist is comfortable with its use. A day-treatment modality is a good place to learn this technique, as the children spend a considerable amount of time in the therapeutic milieu. One can chance an interpretation more readily in this type of intensive setting.

Life Space Interview

As mentioned earlier, the treatment modality used at The Children's Center is eclectic. A technique labeled Life Space Interview (LSI), defined by Fritz Redl as "clinical exploitation of life events and emotional first aid on the spot" (1966, p.42), is our most frequently used treatment modality. LSI techniques are useful in all phases of treatment after a relationship has been established between the children and the therapists.

With an exceptional sense of humor and a lack of professional jargon, Redl explained that this modality is not new but a practical application of dynamic and group work–oriented techniques. He founded and directed the Detroit Group Project, "Pioneer House," a residential facility for teenage delinquent youngsters in the 1950s. At that time, group therapy and individual psychotherapy with acting-out children were not widely used. His work has been described as "providing the fifties with a conceptual screen for viewing all the diverse elements in a therapeutic milieu" (Whittaker, 1979, p. 49). LSI uses the teacher-therapist as a mediator to help children gain an understanding and make connections between their feelings, the action they are taking, and the consequences of it.

The techniques advocated by Redl sound quite easy to carry through, but they demand training and an understanding of how family dynamics affect behavior. LSI interventions are effective only if the therapeutic alliance has been established between the child and therapist and if the children are ready to make changes in their behavior.

The therapists also have to feel good about their ability to use every situation to therapeutic advantage. The idea is not to make children behave but to help them find positive ways to interact, improve their self-esteem, increase their feelings of trust, and develop inner controls.

The age group of children referred to the Center necessitates simplification and reorientation of some concepts within the framework of developmental, behavioral, and cognitive theories. LSI's major strategies are useful with young children, but *only* when a relationship of trust has been established with the therapist. Specific examples of on-the-spot interventions will explain the LSI technique. Consider the following scenario.

The children were sitting around a table with individual balls of clay in front of each of them. They were rolling and punching the clay, having a good time. Carlos (3 years, 6 months of age) sat next to Mary (age 4), who suddenly let out a yell. She had taken a piece of his clay, and he had bitten her. Biting is not acceptable, and Carlos as well as Mary, the aggressor, were removed. The therapist sat between them in the hall, and the following conversation took place:

Therapist: Mary, tell me what happened.

Mary: I needed more clay.

Therapist: What did you do?

Mary: I needed more clay. He bited me.

Therapist: Mary, what did you do?

Mary: I took some of his clay.

Therapist: O.K. What else could you have done instead of taking it?

Mary: (After a long pause) Ask you, get more from the bucket, ask Carlos for some.

Therapist: Right on, Mary. Now, Carlos, tell me what happened.

Carlos: She took my clay. I bited her. I want to go back to group.

Therapist: You wanted your clay ball. But biting is not O.K. What else can you do?

Carlos: I don't like Mary. I want to go back to group ... ask you for more.

Therapist: O.K. Let's go back in and see what you both can make.

Both children acknowledged the reality of the incident; the therapist accepted their feelings but not the conflict resolution. By offering alternative behaviors, the incident was used therapeutically. Redl calls this "reality rub in" (1966, p. 44), explaining that disturbed children have a difficult time realizing their role in conflict situations and are quick to come up with alibis. Mary had been in treatment longer and had a more secure relationship with the therapist. This was helpful in resolving the conflict, as she acted as a model for Carlos.

Had these children been younger and less verbal, nonverbal options, which would have been within their achievement level, would have been offered. Had Carlos not bit but hit, the incident would have been handled in the room, the children separated, and nonverbal alternatives, such as clapping hands or jumping up and down, suggested. Using creative media—clay, water, hammering, bean bag throwing, or tearing of newspapers—is also helpful.

Instructing children to say that they are sorry is not productive and teaches manipulative patterns. In the case quoted above, Carlos's affect was legitimate; the overt behavior was not. Telling children, "Use your words," after they have hit or bitten another child is useless because words lack the physical release and the child might not have words ready to use. It might be helpful to give children usable phrases such as "Lay off," "Cut it out," or "I had it first," using disruptive behavior to therapeutic advantage.

Gains Achieved by Inappropriate Behaviors

Why do children dawdle at snack or lunch time? Do they have trouble swallowing or chewing? Do they dislike the food offered? Observation will give a clue how to handle the situation. Dawdling may gain the therapist's undivided attention while the child finishes. He will have no reason to eat faster if the adult falls into the trap of staying. Rather than remaining with the child, the therapist should move on to the next activity with the other children and verbalize to the dawdler that there are more direct ways to get attention, for example, asking. If the behavior is recognized as oppositional rather than as attention getting, removal of the food should be considered, but only after saying something like "You must not be hungry today." It is very important to tell the child why you are doing what you are doing, rather than just doing it. From the behaviorist's point of view, this is a contamination of the method, but LSI and behavior modification are being combined here. The therapist's action is a behavioral response; the verbalization, an interpretive one. The goal should be to support the healthy part of the ego by helping the children to realize what they are doing and its consequences, and then to suggest more appropriate behaviors.

Ignoring Behavior

Totally ignoring negative behavior in a group situation is risky, particularly with children just beginning to gain inner control. Three-year-olds like to use toilet talk. They are talking about a newly found skill, but they have also learned that adults get upset when children talk about "pee" and "poop." It might be hard to ignore, but it does run its course faster if ignored and a quick change is made to a favorable activity or the singing of nonsense words. The use of primary reinforcers for the nonparticipants is also helpful. Removal of the audience strengthens the controls as does the therapist's or teacher's handling of the incident. But continued ignoring increases some children's anxiety, and it is important that the therapist acts. Total disruption of the group needs to be avoided. Knowledge of young three-year-olds' interest in their bodily functions and their newly gained ability to talk will alert the therapist to provide activities to meet those needs: finger painting and water play, as well as the introduction of nonsense words.

Touch Control

The children are sitting on their rugs in a circle on the floor. The therapist plays a record and reads the words to the story. Johnny wiggles, does arm exercises, and is just about to disrupt the activity. A volunteer sitting in back of him moves a little closer and gently rubs his back or touches his shoulder. Johnny relaxes and listens.

Moving close to the young child who is apt to "lose it" provides the child with support to gain self-control. Sometimes a gentle touch on the child's shoulder has a calming effect. Some children, however, withdraw from touch, particularly if they have been exposed to abuse. With them, touch control has to be used carefully, since it might remind them of earlier experiences when touch meant pain. A safety zone can, at times, be created by setting the child on a chair rather than on a rug piece while listening to a story. It is important to use touch control prior to the disturbance, not afterward; otherwise the child will become totally confused, thinking that his or her negative behavior has been rewarded.

All young children, but particularly those who might have missed closeness and bonding during infancy, need general closeness, touching, being held, being picked up. A rocking chair in the toddler lab is of great help. However, care should be taken not to increase children's helplessness by picking them up during an activity.

Corey, a small 3-year-old with minimal speech, sat during movement therapy while the other children tiptoed around. A volunteer picked him up and carried him into the group. It was pointed out to her that taking Corey's hand is more helpful for his emotional, as well as his large-motor, development. Carrying him increased his helplessness pattern. A few weeks later, he was galloping with the best of them, at the same time beaming about his success.

Humor Is a Lightning Rod

Children are very skillful in setting up power struggles with adults over very small incidents. One can observe such occurrences daily in the grocery store, particularly around 5:30 P.M. It is a challenge not to succumb to authoritarian measures, but to use a sense of humor to save the situation. The same is even more true in a therapy group. It is almost impossible to work with a group of disturbed children without a sense of humor. Humor can diffuse anxiety, save the child from feeling guilty, and allow the therapist to avoid becoming involved in a power struggle. It relieves tension in all concerned and slows down burnout of the teacher or therapist.

Limit Setting

Setting of clearly defined and consistently maintained limits provides an external framework of security and consistency for children who have a weak or totally lacking internal control system. Requests communicated in a matter-of-fact voice tell the children that the adult has high expectations to which they will conform. Limit setting should be couched in positive statements. For example, "Chairs are to sit on," rather than "Don't stand on your chair."

Total permissiveness is not productive in therapy groups, but an overload of rules and regulations should be avoided. Rules such as "We don't hurt people," "We don't break things on purpose," and "We don't ever run out of the building" are easily understood by children and adults so that their consistent enforcement is not difficult. The ultimate goal is for the child to internalize external controls.

"I Can't Do It"

Practical success experiences like starting a project or finishing it are important. Assisting a child who is frustrated by a task can prevent frustration-induced misbehavior and allow the child to "hurdle" the assignment and succeed. A few words to the volunteer, like "Jenny is learning to hold scissors. Please help her get started," might do the trick. Help should come only at the beginning; the child, not the therapist or volunteer, needs to learn to cut.

To Summarize

The second phase of treatment, stretching over several months, is the most important one in this treatment model. It is demanding on the child and the therapist. The children gain and intensify internal controls through the use of a variety of verbal communication techniques, like LSI. They gain self-confidence in managing conflict situations with peers and frequently have a brand new experience in attachment to an adult. The therapist reflects and interprets behavior, thus beginning to lead the children to independent problem solving.

Establishment of a therapeutic alliance is the major aim of Phase

Two. The move from looking at observable behavior to looking for reasons to explain it is taking place. This leap demands trust in the adult, willingness to change on the children's part, and the families' cooperation.

The therapeutic alliance is established by offering the child security in routines, limit setting, and modeling. Increasing self-esteem and a greater behavioral repertory lay the foundation for the use of reflection, interpretation, and LSI. These methods have been found to be the most appropriate tools to achieve the desired goals of internalizing controls, decreasing anxiety, and increasing age-appropriate functioning in young children.

Intrinsic rewards have taken the place of primary reinforcers, communication skills improve, and peer relationships are formed. The therapist is using understanding of family dynamics and insight rather than behavioral interventions to achieve the desired goals. The child is encouraged to recognize the connection between feelings and actions and consequences. The mediator helps in crystallizing all three and aids the child in resolving conflicts. In time, usually during the third treatment phase, the child recognizes that this process leads to a happier, less conflict-laden life.

PHASE THREE OF THE TREATMENT PROCESS

While the first phase was to observe, and the second one to explore, the third phase is to solidify the gains made. The children are now ready to experiment with their newly gained feelings, actions and consequences, and the role adults can play in helping them in this endeavor. They reach out to other group members, participate in program planning, and become more independent.

Phases of treatment are not distinct entities. At times children slide back from one level to the other. Improved behavior is not maintained consistently. First, the improvement is noted a day at a time, then over several days, and finally for weeks. The children are now free to use all their abilities and often surprise the therapists with their insight. They raise a fist, but instead of hitting, they say, "Quit it."

The Children

The children's cognitive functioning improves. Their lengthened attention span and improved frustration tolerance lead to better task persistence and, at times, higher IQ scores than on admission testing. Projective tests indicate their increased self-esteem and trust in the world. The older children particularly enjoy being group members and respond to peer pressure.

The children have become freer, walk straighter, maintain eye contact, and form friendships with each other. Let's look at Mark again.

Mark's behavior in group continued to improve. He made friends, came up with good ideas, and related well to the therapists. The treatment goals established on admission came closer to being completed. Behavior at daycare also improved, and he was able to assume some leadership positions there. Mark realized that all adults were working together and agreed to invite his day-care worker to come and see the Center.

Behavior at home remained a problem. Though Mark's tantrums had disappeared, he now openly challenged family members with expression of his feelings. They, in turn, called this "back talk," and conflict ensued, which confused him and set him back. He felt unloved at home, and Mondays proved to be very difficult.

The tantrums had completely disappeared, but Mark now challenged the therapist in more sophisticated ways than previously. He cleverly tried to sabotage the therapist's program planning. When the therapist brought out instant pudding, Mark started, "Today we want to make soup not pudding, right guys? That's baby food." His leadership was not criticized, his behavior not interpreted, but reality testing and legitimatizing were used. The therapist responded with, "Great idea, but what are we going to use for soup? I did not bring anything. Did you, Mark, or Johnny? What do we need and can we bring it tomorrow? You all plan it, and I'll bring what you assign me, okay?" The therapist thus avoided contagion of negative behavior, and the activity proceeded.

Mark's behavior at home and in daycare improved as the family's handling of his problems improved. Discharge testing showed an increase in self-esteem and the ability to solve problems in a more acceptable manner. He was discharged after eight months of treatment and, according to follow-up reports, is doing well.

By this phase, self-esteem has improved, along with the children's sense of humor and cognitive functioning. They take pride in their work and make suggestions for activities. Alternative behavior patterns have become habitual, verbal interactions are substituted for physical cues, and feelings are labeled more freely and accurately.

The children's play is now more focused. They have more fun, ask more questions, and develop a greater awareness of their surroundings. They also form friendships and tolerate stress better. The children's vocabulary has increased, which leads to greater verbal facility and more group discussion.

The Therapists

During this phase the therapists remain important as models, and the children often express their positive feelings toward them quite openly. Positive feelings play a greater role, and with the therapists' leadership the children become more interested in and kinder to each other. They can now label feelings and, under the therapists' guidance, explore them. The therapists step back and encourage the children to assume more responsibility for problem resolutions. The therapists reflect and interpret behaviors and remind the children of useful alternatives, thus leading the children to independent problem solving within accepted group norms.

The Atmosphere in the Group

A group containing mostly children in the third phase of treatment might look, most of the time, like a rather well-adjusted group of preschool children. Such a group occurs only rarely, as children are discharged as soon as their treatment goals are achieved. Due to the continuous pressure of new arrivals, discharge is, at times, too early. Some children react to this negatively, returning to earlier behavior patterns in order to assure themselves continuation of treatment. Some individual time with their therapists, and discussion of their successes and the changes they have made, is usually helpful and leads to prideful acceptance of graduation.

Program

For five-year-olds who will be discharged to enter regular kindergarten, readiness work is stressed. Many children with emotional problems and disabilities show poor small-motor coordination. Paper-and-pencil practice is important because academic readiness will be expected from them. A longer attention span for stories with more words and fewer pictures, active participation, and the finishing of projects are stressed. The projects are longer and usually have a connecting theme like songs, stories, and music covering the same topic. Transitions go more smoothly.

Interventions

Interventions are quite individually focused and based on the same strategies as were used during the second phase. Some of the children can verbalize interpretations independently, indicating some internalization of the concepts. Verbalization of feelings is forthcoming, resulting in longer conversations with therapists. The alternative behaviors suggested are now more appreciated and used with greater frequency at home and in the neighborhood.

SPECIFIC PROBLEMS

Early Discharge

Many children are referred only a few months prior to their entrance into kindergarten. There is usually not enough time to help them adequately, for they frequently show severe behavior problems. It is a frustrating experience for staff, and a failure experience for the children, if discharge has to occur due to age.

At times, family crises, like imprisonment of one or the other parent, the coming and going of live-in companions, unwanted pregnancies, illnesses, loss of employment, evictions, trouble with welfare agencies, remarriage, and a myriad of other crises, stop progress in the child's treatment for a short time. However, the group has become a safe place for the children; they are able to express their feelings and, on occasion, make greater progress in a time of crisis. Close cooperation between parent and child therapists is especially important during crisis times.

Changes in staff may also cause periodic regression. Therapists leave to enter graduate school, take higher-paying jobs, get married, or have babies. It is almost always seen by children as desertion and rejection. Old behavior patterns reappear; limit testing and negative behaviors increase, as if the child is saying, "I am rejecting you before you can do it to me." The therapeutic alliance and the establishment of trust help in overcoming these hurdles, however.

Toward the end of the second phase or the beginning of the third phase, parents may withdraw their child from treatment if he or she has made progress. They may feel that because the child has dropped the behavior that had distressed them, he or she is ready to be discharged. They thank the staff profusely but rarely listen to their statements regarding the need for continuation of treatment. The child, who has enjoyed coming to the Center, will feel punished for having changed and will regress to earlier behavior patterns. In these instances, joint parent-child sessions conducted by parent therapists are helpful.

Out of a myriad of cases referred to The Children's Center, let me select one more that personifies the problems of working with young, emotionally disturbed children.

Jason, a very small, appealing, big-eyed, 4-year-old boy, was brought to the Center in diapers. Referral problems were encopresis, running away from home, and overdependency on the father. In preschool, poor play skills and helplessness patterns were observed. He had been totally toilet trained but regressed at the time of his younger sister's birth one year prior to admission.

Financial problems in the family necessitated the mother's going to work and Jason's admission to a day-care center. His remaining at daycare and, thus, his mother's job were seriously threatened by his behavior.

On admission, a behavioral program was begun. Independent trips to the bathroom were rewarded with a spoonful of ice cream; this yielded increased trips, but the encopresis did not diminish. The social consequences of his soiling became evident to him, and he withdrew in a corner rather than using the toilet. Jason tried to force the therapists to recommend discharge so that mother would have to stay home and care for him. As primary reinforcers did not work with him, it was decided to break his cycle of dependency and helplessness and let him take care of himself when he soiled.

When he had a bowel movement in his pants, he was given clean underwear, taken out of the room, and asked to change. Jason objected strenuously to this routine, expecting to be wiped and taken care of. When mother agreed to the same procedure at home, incidents became rarer.

Though he sometimes entered the playroom without pants, he slowly realized that the staff meant business, and rewards at that time became effective. They fortunately also came from the children, who began to include him in cooperative play, since he did not spend so much time in the bathroom anymore and smelled better.

He easily understood the natural consequences of his behavior and made some progress in toilet training. But he seemed to use intermittent reinforcement on staff by going to the bathroom regularly for a week, only to regress again the following week. The same behavior appeared at home and in daycare. Parent therapy revealed serious problems at home: the father's repeated absences, open quarrels, and threats of separation.

Progress continued in all other areas; Jason became a leader in his group. Though his accidents became more sporadic, they still persisted. Jason was better able to handle free play, and his skill level increased. In the meantime, his father had left the home and visited only irregularly. Jason was able to mention this to his therapist.

During the third phase of treatment, the decision was made to provide Jason with a male individual therapist for the last three months in the group and during the summer prior to entering kindergarten. Jason related well within a short time, was able to bring up his hurt about his father's leaving and his hope that if he were to become "sick" again, his father would return.

Joint therapy sessions with the mother and Jason improved their relationship and helped her to understand her little son's problem. Rather than perpetuating his problem, keeping him helpless and infantile, Jason's mother stressed some of his positive competencies. Jason entered a preschool for an extra year and then kindergarten. At last report, he had maintained his progress.

The combination of treatment modalities worked well in this case.

Discharge can be traumatic for children as well as therapists. They have to leave their safe world, the friends they have made, and the environment that has protected them and given them strength. It is this strength that is stressed when discharge time comes. Earlier behaviors are described, and child and therapist jointly go through the steps of changes made. Graduation parties with hats and cake are a definite step for the children who have needed early intensive psychotherapy. They have formed attachments and gained trust, which enables them to function better in the world at large.

To help them with the transition to the larger system, they receive follow-up services in day-care centers and the public school system.

In Summary

While behavior modification was used in Phase One and dynamic principles applied to treatment in Phase Two, the third phase cements the changes made through some of the interventions used earlier. The therapist becomes an even stronger model, and peer influence increases. The children's understanding of the connection between feelings, actions, and consequences is deepened, and many are now able to verbalize this. Other children remain unable to do this, though their behavior has improved to the point that conflicts have become rarer and solutions come easier. Various case studies have illustrated the most salient strategies used within the eclectic model that has been described.

Peers and the group assume greater importance. The children rely more on their peers' opinions, work together in groups, and gain enjoyment in learning and completing more complicated projects.

Young children, particularly, are not ever seen in a vacuum. Their small world, their family, is but a microcosm of the larger world surrounding them. Both areas are full of tension, struggles, and anxieties that influence their lives and their behavior. Our hope is that they will enter the great, exciting, but often hostile world in better shape than when they entered The Children's Center.

Phases of treatment very often do not proceed according to schedule, and it is difficult to generalize about a time frame, as young children's lives are totally dependent upon their environment.

While theories and strategies are the skeleton of the treatment program, the activities discussed in the next chapter put the meat and flesh on it.

Chapter 7
Activities

INTRODUCTION

Programming is only a means to an end, not an end in itself. As discussed previously, activities form the backbone of this intervention model; their selection demands knowledge of the developmental process and the cognitive, physical, and emotional functioning level of each child in the group. This is partially established by the psychological assessment and by the developmental and family histories taken prior to admission. However, observation of the child in the group adds another important dimension. This is particularly true for overactive children who are able to maintain attention in a one-to-one testing session but become overstimulated in a group.

Michael, age 3, was referred by his day-care worker and his mother for hyperactivity and noncompliance. They both wondered about the use of medication. He lived with a younger sister and his single mother in the maternal grandparents' home. The mother was attending training sessions to gain self-sufficiency, and Michael was in daycare from 7 A.M. to 5:30 P.M. At home Michael was demanding and hard to discipline by his mother and grandparents; in daycare he was aggressive toward peers and adults, and his level of cognitive ability was questioned. He used many sound substitutions, making his speech difficult to understand.

During the evaluation Michael remained in his seat, was spontaneous, attentive, and maintained good eye contact. Use of a nonverbal, performance-type IQ measure revealed a child with advanced small-motor coordination, persistence in problem solving, and a tendency to control. When permitted to make choices, he was easily redirected. Administration of a visual storytelling test was less productive. Michael looked at the pictures, but his responses were not understandable. Referral problems were not apparent. He seemed to enjoy the attention and approval given and responded well to praise. His mother, observing the testing through a one-way window, was astonished at his behavior.

Admission to group therapy with special emphasis on speech therapy was recommended. Michael's first few weeks in group were difficult. He flitted from toy to toy, grabbed toys he wanted, and did not relate to peers or adults. He progressed well in individual speech therapy sessions, beginning to use speech rather than physical means to relate to peers. With special attention to his strength, to structure, and to success experiences, his activity level decreased, his aggression lessened, and he was able to relate to peers. Parent and grandparents attended a parenting class, and they as well as the day-care provider reported slow but steady changes in Michael's behavior.

What will the children gain from certain activities? Increased self-esteem, specific skills, relationships with peers and adults, and enjoyment of success. What will the therapist, day-care worker, or teacher learn about the children? Their level of functioning, ability to relate, and strengths and weaknesses in a variety of areas.

GOALS

Activities need to increase children's self-esteem and widen their cognitive, physical, and emotional repertory; they also need to be fun. What must the therapist or day-care worker do to achieve these goals? A few general principles have been established: The shorter the children's attention span, the greater their anxiety; the poorer their impulse control, the more they hurt; therefore, the tighter the program has to be.

Tight programming means having material ready that is age-appropriate, appealing, and varied; it also means establishing a daily routine. It provides direction, helps to develop internal controls, and gives the children concrete experiences within a time frame. Knowing what to expect makes it easier to concentrate on the task at hand, provides structure in an unobtrusive way, and helps the therapist in preparing the day's program.

The program for each day is structured to achieve short- and long-term goals. A short-term goal is measurable. The short-term goal for Michael, for example, was to learn five words a week and play for five minutes with one other child. The long-term goal was to form positive relationships with peers and adults. The time spent on each activity, the specific materials used, and the theme are different for each age group and depend on the skill level of the children, their age, and their functioning level. Quiet activities follow active ones, cognitive challenges are interspersed with music and movement. Food is used for relaxation, the teaching of self-care skills, and social interchange. Nonverbal, creative activities help children have success experiences and are used extensively to express both positive and negative feelings. Play in its various forms is one of the mainstays of activity therapy for young children, since play is their forum for learning intellectual as well as social skills.

TRANSITIONS

Transitions from one activity to another are difficult for most children, but particularly for those with behavior problems. The controlling, acting-out child uses this opportunity to start running around, refusing to clean up and to join the next activity. The timid child, who is more comfortable remaining in the current activity, fights change. This child might clean up but then remains distant from the group. Both the timid and the acting-out child fight change, one out of fear of failure, the other to create chaos.

Transitions demand careful planning. For example, outside time is followed by snack, an activity that lures almost all children off the trikes and away from the sandbox. With more than one adult interacting with each group of children, one begins the next activity while the other helps the children put away the toys with which they have been playing. Picking up one hundred Lego pieces from the floor looks like and is an overwhelming job. The experienced therapist or volunteer will reduce the quantity to fifty pieces before the children have the opportunity to dump them or will bring in a dustpan to sweep them up—usually to everybody's delight.

DAILY PROGRAM

A productive day consists of storytime, playtime, cognitive skills development, large- and small-motor activities, snack, alternately language, music, or a movement activity, and a creative activity. To structure the day is important, but special conditions at times necessitate flexibility in the daily schedule.

STORYTIME

The day's activities begin with storytime. It is surprising how many children cannot respond to the question, "Why do we have books?" After a lengthy bus ride to the Center, children often find entering the group difficult. Being ready to talk or actually talking about a book that the child has picked is a success experience, permitting closeness to an adult and providing peace. The selection of a specific book of particular significance to the child starts the day off well.

Books must be age-appropriate in content, length, and appearance. What happens if books are too advanced? The children lose interest and start unacceptable behaviors; the positive value of reading is lost. Books for younger children should be carefully picked: Large pictures, short texts, and familiar material enable the child to identify with them. It is helpful to cut out large pictures, paste them on cardboard, and write a few short sentences on the back so that the child can simultaneously listen and look. Pictures can be cut out of torn books, and abbreviated texts can be used. Sitting next to either side of the adult provides the closeness frequently needed. Not all books should have a moral, such as angry animals or harmless monsters. Clouds and skies and stories about different people are fun. Older children might like to read about things they hear about all the time: airplanes, spaceships, dinosaurs, bears, or issues that widen their horizons.

It is hard to read and look at children at the same time. Many teachers and therapists, particularly in the younger groups, like to tell stories rather than read them. This permits eye contact and often lengthens the children's attention span.

PLAY

General

Much has been written about play, and various opinions exist concerning its worth. Over the years the role of play in preschool education has undergone many changes. The curriculum vacillated from play only to an emphasis on academics, like French and reading at age three, experts apparently being unable to decide whether children learn through play activities or only from academic instruction. Fortunately, we now know that children learn a great deal through play and that the preschool years are the best time to kindle an interest in learning. Such learning must be encouraged by parents and teachers and based on children's natural curiosity, their unconventional imagination, and their delight in experimentation. They need time to experiment, to create, and to have fun.

Many early childhood educators now agree that play for young children is like work for adults. It serves as an instrument of learning, of growth, of satisfaction, of social interaction, and of establishing the child's individuality. Play consolidates learning in specific steps, serves cognitive processes, and provides a way to bring mastery over anxieties and conflicts. Brian Sutton-Smith has written extensively on play, describing its historical origin and concluding that "play is neither good nor bad. Like language or music, it is a form of expression and communication. What makes it good or bad is what we do with it" (Sutton-Smith, 1985, p. 65).

Play follows some rather definite progression: Infants' and toddlers' play is usually exploratory, solitary, and repetitive. Blocks are piled and knocked over, only to be piled and knocked over again. Cups are filled and emptied again and again, accompanied by joyous laughter.

The three-year-old often moves to parallel play, beginning to use play as a form of communication. Playing next to another child rather than with him or her is the beginning of the realization that companionship can be rewarding. Many children with special needs remain in isolated play situations, indicating their inability to relate, their fear of rejection, their fear of risking.

Interactive play, the next stage, consists of nothing more than pushing a small car back and forth to another child, but this in time develops to the building of a road, taking turns, thereby truly becoming cooperative play. During this stage children help each other, change roles, follow the lead of another child, and freely share and borrow materials.

Children's approach to play materials may range from hesitant, fearful, or distant to bold, curious, or exploratory, each providing a clue to their feelings about themselves. For instance, the choice of the material itself is telling: Is it nonstructured, like paint or clay; preordained, like a puzzle; or completely noncreative, like tracing or copying? Similarly, we gain an understanding of the child by his or her selection of a playmate. Is it always the same, and who? The most aggressive one? The one without language? The same sex or the opposite? The smallest or the leader? Does the child use pretend play to show identification with the same or opposite sex parent, peer, or sibling?

The atmosphere in the room, it is hoped, is relaxed and ready for fun; the space is open, but not too large, and the materials are varied. The adults enjoy play, either entering in or staying out, but making their presence felt.

Play is important for all children, but particularly for children with special needs. They have already indicated their difficulties in an inappropriate fashion and must be provided with alternative forms of expression.

Play also serves as direct, nonverbal communication to compensate for frustrating experiences, defeat, and failure. Reality and fantasy are sometimes hard to distinguish, and pretend games of four- and five-year-olds are rich in content and meaning. Pretend play is an important step in social development, permitting the acting out of real concerns. Major changes have taken place in children's play because of changed social roles. Girls are now doctors rather than nurses, garbage truck drivers, and carpenters. These role changes in girls seem to be more frequent than in boys, who only rarely elect to be secretaries or even teachers.

Pretend Play

Make-believe play most frequently occurs between the ages of three and five as children become more curious about real and unreal and have mastered mobility and language. "Let's pretend" play is important in social and intellectual development, particularly since fairy tales have been moved to the back of the bookshelf. It also tells who the child wants to be and how this person is seen.

Role playing initiated by children can solve everyday problems, prepare children for real-life situations, offset some frustrations, express needs, and imitate important adults. Children often act out their anxieties and permit a glimpse into their world, which then, in turn, can be used in helping them to understand it. A doll corner with a stove, a cupboard, dishes, and a small table and chairs allows children to recreate family situations that often reveal a child's problem and can help in handling it. Participation of the teacher-therapist can be on different levels. To a child who has thrown the new baby in the imaginary garbage can, an offhand remark such as "Sometimes it's hard to have a new baby at home" might be reassuring. And rather than interrupting the play, an avenue of discourse can be opened. If a child creates a play situation of a mother holding a baby and another child standing on the sidelines, a more direct response such as "What could this little person over here do to be picked up also?" might be appropriate. The same play might also give the child an opportunity to show positive "mothering." Research has shown, however, that children at times combine remembered and imaginary events, bedtime stories and TV shows, and mix them up into one sequence. It is essential to take imaginary play at face value.

Doll play, unfortunately, is often limited to girls, thus depriving boys of the opportunity to show positive feelings. Boys assume roles of Superman, He-Man, or other macho characters shown on TV, but only rarely see affection expressed. A whole flock of "Batmen" might be running around the playground, black capes flying in the wind. A goal might be to legitimize such play into group action and bring it to a successful close. Individual fights between characters like Batman and The Joker should, if possible, be avoided. "Good guy and bad guy" play is not as frequent with preschoolers as with latency-age children and theoretically permits the child to experiment with "moral identities" (Bettelheim, 1987, p. 46).

The designation of the Indian as the "bad guy," rather frequent in the American West, easily leads to problems if Native American children are in the group. It helps to talk about racial differences, read related stories with a different emphasis, or bring in some native materials to explain a different culture.

Free Play

In the course of a day, many of the activities used at The Children's Center focus on play, none as telling and important as free play. Observers sometimes consider free play too "messy" and disorderly. The lack of structure, which is purposeful, might appear as a lack of control or poor planning or no planning by the adults in charge. Far from the truth!

Free play helps the child to develop initiative, form new friendships, try out ideas, discover new uses for old toys, and, most of all, learn to risk, to experiment. Disturbed children frequently cannot function during free play; their play is stereotyped and repetitive, often consisting only of lining up cars or racing trucks at breakneck speed. Their play remains unfocused and disorganized, leading to a high activity level and often ending in conflict situations. Many of the children, overwhelmed by the riches of choice, lack experience and confidence to be creative and imaginative.

Depending on the composition of the group, free play may be totally free or partially structured. The "partial structure" consists, for example, of a Fisher Price garage, clay or playdough, or puzzles, thus avoiding the disintegration of a group composed of children with a high level of activity and a low inner focus of control. Particularly on Monday morning, a shorter free play period with only certain toys proves helpful. Returning to the Center on Mondays, many of the children show the effect of weekends spent in dysfunctional surroundings. One hundred Lego pieces will remind them of the confusing surroundings they have just left. Structure is needed to assure them of security.

Structured Group Play

Many children with special needs are overwhelmed with their own needs and demands and, most of all, with a feeling of not getting their share. When all these feelings are crowded inside, it is difficult to be creative. A little help can go a long way. Materials can be available to play supermarket: cottage cheese and milk cartons, empty cake boxes, wax fruit, unopened cans, play money, a cash register, and price tags made by the children—the group is ready to compete with any grocery store. Or how about going to McDonald's? Paper cups, placemats, napkins, clay hamburgers, saucers, and plates. Who will be the cashier? The customers?

Doctor's bag? But more than just the doctor, who will be the nurse? The patient? Sign the bill? There is something for everybody to do.

A train ride or plane trip to New York, or better yet, Africa? The pilot and engineer need caps. Who will be the stewards, the ground crew, the flight controller?

And then there is always just plain dress up: hats, ties, maybe a mustache and a beard for the boys; high-heeled shoes for the young ladies, long, lacy skirts, and handbags. How about a little wig? The possibilities are endless.

GROUP ACTIVITIES

Not all activities are play. Children need to learn that work can be fun, but that it requires attention, persistence, and the willingness to try something new even if it results in failure. This is very difficult for many children, particularly for those with problems, because failures have been their mainstay. Therefore, learning activities have to be carefully selected based on the functioning level of each child rather than on age. Individual differences need to be kept in mind and used skillfully. One child will need activities that promise immediate rewards and few rules, and that can be done alone or with one other child. In contrast, another child can continue with a project tomorrow, is a "groupie," and likes to be told what to do. It is a question not of good or bad, bright or dull, but of individual differences.

Vitner (1974) has devised a most useful scheme of classification of activities for children, dividing them into six categories according to high or low prescriptiveness, control, physical movement, competency, rewards, and interaction.

1. *Prescriptiveness* denotes the degree and range of rules in an activity. For example, in cooking, the recipe must be followed or Jell-O won't set; in a puzzle, the pieces must be placed in a specific way or they won't fit. Water play, on the other hand, has only a few rules.
2. *Control* means the level of supervision. Playing ball has a high control level, while looking at a book has a low one.
3. *Physical movement* is the extent to which action is permitted or required. Riding a trike can be contrasted to playing with clay.
4. *Competency* describes the skills required for performance. To cut, a child must know how to hold scissors. Tearing does not require this skill.

5. *Rewards* are integral to certain activities like the creation of a painting, while waiting for Jell-O to set demands delayed gratification.
6. *Interaction* describes involvement with others. It's hard to talk on the phone by one's self, but no interaction is required when listening to stories or riding a sled.

Not all activities can be pigeonholed within these parameters, but they do provide a framework of useful classification (see Appendix E).

Cognitive Skill Acquisition

Children need to acquire information, organize it, and then use it appropriately in problem-solving situations. Verbal and nonverbal reasoning has to be taught in imaginative ways. Sensorimotor activities come first in children's development. Babies suck, squeeze, and touch whatever object they can get hold of. By age two, children discriminate, differentiate, and begin to classify. Within the next few years, children learn to sort and match. Finally, they name objects generically.

The Sense of Sight

Children can sort objects according to size, color, and shape. Is this button large, red, and round, or small, blue, and square? This activity can be extended by asking the children to find something round in the room, like wheels, balloons, a picture of the sun, cups, paper plates, a button. Or glasses, eyes, flowers, oranges, apples, and potatoes can be discussed. How about square shapes: books, napkins, blocks, toys, packages? Or rectangles: windows, beds, pictures. And triangles like roofs. Show them a large ball, a box—the more concrete, the better.

Sight can teach the expression of feelings. Often children with emotional problems will smile while hitting a child and deny being angry when the emotion is labeled. A trip to the mirror to produce visual images of these emotions teaches children to recognize their anger. Labeling might lead to denial, whereas seeing and modeling might be convincing.

The next step can be drawing out similarities and differences. How is a snap different from a hook, a banana from a green pepper? And how are they alike? Concepts like same and different or analogies are frequent tasks on intelligence tests and demand a certain sophistication that many young children do not have. Most children, who have watched "Sesame Street," are aware of basic shapes. They can name the shape of an object but not describe its use. Yes, an orange is round, but what do you do with it? Teaching by sight needs to be taken a step further, incorporating function.

The Sense of Touch

With young children, teaching is best done as concretely as possible. How do things feel? An orange feels different from a banana, sandpaper different from silk. It is easier to teach concepts like bumpy and smooth, and short and long, if the child can feel objects, so that concreteness replaces abstractions. Does plastic feel different from wood? A selection of objects can be put into a small paper bag. Pick a pair that feels the same, one that feels different. The children can then be blindfolded, one at a time, and asked to pull out a piece of fur or wood. Children afraid of a blindfold can just close their eyes. Liquid and solid is a little harder to demonstrate, but asking a child to take hold of water in contrast to a block will make the concept understandable.

The Sense of Smell

Children can learn by using their sense of smell. Vinegar smells different from apple juice, French fries from tomatoes. Thus, labeling becomes a game, a learning experience, fun. Why are these exercises important? They teach concepts, lengthen attention span, make learning an adventure—all in all, sharpen cognitive skills.

The Sense of Taste

Sorting by taste is a popular activity. The children will love to differentiate between sweet and sour, hot and cold, liquid and solid, soft and chewy, bland and spicy. Remember, it will take repetition, but there is plenty of time in a day, and it might take less time than photocopying pictures of apples and bananas!!

The Sense of Sound

The terms *inside voice* and *outside voice* are used all the time and are a useful differentiation, but again, they can be made concrete with a whisper and a shout! How about the sound of a guitar and a horn? A drum and a cymbal? Turning your back to the children, you can let them guess which one you are using. They can take turns with the instruments, and records can be used for the sounds that animals and vehicles make.

Classifying, Sorting by Function

Sorting by function works as well. A pitcher is to pour, a glass is to drink, an orange is to eat. Is it a vegetable, fruit, or meat? Gloves, shoes, socks, sweaters, and T-shirts all have specific functions that need to be taught. A shoe fits on a foot; a mitten or glove, on a hand. Where do you wear a hat? How are these functions similar? How about a chair, a bench, or a sofa? A bed or a crib? You might want to use doll furniture at first, then move on to pictures, and finally to verbalization.

Preacademic Skills

Writing letters and numbers requires skills that are based on visual perceptual motor development. The shape of a letter needs to be perceived, a visual image retained, and the form then executed through motor involvement. This is a complicated process that frequently needs to be broken into parts before a child is able to complete it. According to many theoreticians, perceptions are measured in reference to one's own body, which then, in turn, makes it essential to recognize boundaries. Concepts such as *in front of, beside, behind*, or *in back of* are very difficult for many children to grasp. To regulate the movements of fingers, legs, and parts of bodies in specific directions, particularly at the same time, demands repetition. Until children grasp laterality, *b* and *d* will look alike, directions will not be meaningful, and confusion might easily result. Lying on the back and pedaling in the air help with bilateral coordination, swinging of arms with directionality. Rolling, bouncing, and tossing a ball to a simple melody further eye-hand coordination, a sense of rhythm, and social adjustment—all three in one. With practice, ego-alien motions can become ego-syntonic, increasing a child's positive body image and improving spatial relations. Many children struggle when simultaneous auditory and visual stimuli are presented, which adds to their feeling of helplessness and failure, increases their anxiety, and contributes to their presumed hyperactivity.

Preacademic skills such as counting, matching colors, sequencing, learning the alphabet, and recognizing letters and numbers will be needed for kindergarten. It is essential, however, to present these activities in a challenging and concrete way before abstractness can be expected. Colors can be taught by naming those of socks, shoes, or shirts of the children in group. The activity can then be expanded to counting all the blues and reds or finding matching colored objects in the room.

Singing the alphabet is fine, but children respond well when it is broken down in sets of three or four letters, rather than expecting the child to remember all twenty-six! Recognition of letters can begin with teaching the first letter of the child's name and then repeating it on pictures and the lunch box. It is helpful to expand on the same letter, like Mary and milk, Curtis and crackers, Jason and jam. Some children with very low self-esteem refuse to write their name; they can write any other letter connected with a meaningful activity or a food. Teaching the alphabet might also be done by collecting pictures of things and pinning them up underneath the letter, on a clothesline, or taping them on cork strips.

Large-Motor Activities

Many children show major strength outdoors. They often play more cooperatively, try newly learned skills, and are more comfortable. Yet others appear more fearful and stay close to the door, communicating their need for the structure of four walls to be at ease.

Regardless of how they approach it, playing outside is a favorite activity of most young children. They are so pleased with their newly acquired ability of locomotion that they can hardly wait to use it. Snow or shine, outside time is essential.

John, age 4, loved to play outdoors. He could outrun, outpedal, and throw a ball farther than any other child in his day-care group. His language was hard to understand, and once inside, he did not enter into group activities and withdrew from his peers. His intellectual ability was questioned. He did like to listen to stories but rarely picked a book. Given a leadership role in large-motor abilities outdoors, transferring some of it indoors during movement therapy, John improved in self-esteem and was able to function age-appropriately in all areas.

Children develop their large-motor coordination through pedaling trikes, climbing on the monkey bars, or just running up and down a hill. Observing their imagination and ability in playing in the sandbox, their laterality in throwing a ball, their anxiety or fearlessness in coming down the slide, or even their tendency to self-destruct in dangerous no-hands activities elucidates their strength or their weakness. The wading pool is a neverending source of new observations. Some children will not change into suits, some won't go in, some won't come out. Many games such as Duck Duck Goose, Hide-and-Seek, and Red Rover teach the social skills of cooperation, taking turns, being last, and losing. Overall, outdoor activities aid in releasing energy, providing a badly needed outlet for active preschoolers.

Movement Activities

Movement activities help children experience their own bodies, as well as learn about spatial relationships and balance. How far can my arm reach? How does it feel to walk on my heels? Using movement as an indoor group activity has proven to be an important avenue for achieving changes in withdrawn children's behavior. The freedom of expression seems to loosen some of their inhibitions, and the new behavior then generalizes to other areas. The movements are not prescribed, as in dance or calisthenics, but encourage free rhythmic expression of feelings, usually to music. No verbalization and very little compliance with rules are demanded. Though many children, particularly boys, join in hesitantly at first, in a short time they look forward to the movement therapist's weekly visits.

Small-Motor Activities

A great deal of time should be spent daily on small-motor activities. Many children have trouble using their small muscles and would much rather run and jump than sit at the table and struggle with holding a pencil. However, it is essential for children to become comfortable with scissors and pencils prior to entering kindergarten. Children who cannot cut can learn to tear paper, which will assist in developing the same muscles needed for cutting later on. Newspaper is easiest to tear and usually readily available. Opening pea pods and stringing beads demand the same pincer movement required for pencil dexterity and cutting. By varying the tasks, opposition to them might be reduced.

Some children are ambidextrous, so the "good" hand needs to be identified by tabulating for at least one week which hand the child uses for eating, hitting, shaking hands, or reaching. This can be called the "good hand" and its use rewarded verbally, while the child's usage of the other hand is overlooked. Parents can use the same technique, and no more forceful method should be used to establish laterality.

It is very important that children learn to enjoy small-motor activities, which are difficult and require practice. Vertical lines seem to be easiest for most children to draw; then by about age three and one-half, youngsters advance to horizontal lines and circles. The transition from drawing circles to drawing squares is difficult, but five-year-olds should be able to make corners. Beginning with tracing can give them a boost. It is not advisable to hand children photocopied patterns for cutting or coloring. Such activities destroy their individuality, hamper their creativity, and bore them to boot. Making dots gives direction to children when they are learning to draw more complex designs or letters and numbers. Magic markers are prettier than pencils or crayons, just as newsprint is softer than drawing paper.

Tinker toys and Lego building blocks are fun and helpful in developing eye-hand and motor coordination.

Language Activities: "Talk Is a Four-Letter Word"

Many activities and most social interactions are based on verbal communication. For many children—particularly those who developed speech late, lack fluency, have a limited vocabulary, and frequently use sound substitutions—speech activities are essential. Communication difficulties are most frequently the result of hearing problems; children who do not have normal hearing cannot distinguish differences between sounds and have difficulty repeating them correctly. Language use is dependent on hearing, and evaluation for speech and language problems should be performed by speech pathologists and audiology experts as early as possible.

Most experts agree that children's receptive speech should enable them to identify body parts and use a few simple words by eighteen months. Development of speech is very dependent on the child's environment, and many children who have had limited life experiences, whose use and hearing of language has been restricted to need or emotionally loaded content, show handicaps in that area.

Children of different ethnic groups whose primary language had not been English have similar problems and need special input.

Children who are difficult to understand or who speak only rarely are at a great disadvantage. If not understood by other children or adults, they become easily frustrated and physically combative. Thus, clearness of speech, proper volume, and an adequate vocabulary are essential for social interaction and learning to read and spell.

Teaching of words per se may often not hold children's attention, but concrete objects plus the word might do it. All situations need to be used to extend children's vocabulary. For example, time spent outside can teach phrases and words such as *high, come down, fast, slow, turn around, push, pedal, tunnels,* and *splash.* New words used in the context of a fun activity may be learned more easily than in a structured speech therapy session.

Groups of words can be presented by function, for example, car, bus, airplane, train; or by food groups, for example, apple, banana, pear, orange; or by feelings, for example, happy, sad, grumpy, angry. Combining them with stories, pictures, and concrete objects is helpful. Field trips yield a great deal of material for discussion. Children are interested in words that rhyme and in nursery rhymes, even if they do not understand their meaning. It is important to respond to children's questions in whole sentences; that will give them the idea of sentence patterns. Verbal input in concrete situations helps children to understand the meaning of words, storing them in memory, and then to use the same words to express their own ideas. Let the children dictate letters and read them back to them.

Some children have good speech but do not communicate. This might be due to a variety of reasons, like low self-esteem, fear of making a mistake, having been told, "Silence is golden" or "Don't say anything unless it is nice." A relaxed atmosphere in the group and being assured of acceptance by teacher, parent, or therapist helps the children to gain confidence to express themselves.

Mute children should not be urged to talk, as it may increase their withholding pattern. The dynamics of their muteness must be understood before intervention techniques are used. It is frequently an expression of hostility and anger, and these children must be given other means to express their feelings rather than being pushed to talk.

Music

Many children adore musical activities, whether active or passive. Singing simple melodies with familiar words is a favorite, while songs that combine action (hand clapping) with words are fun for young children and combine motor coordination with listening and language skills. Involvement in musical activities to a large degree depends on the teacher's skill, interest, and enthusiasm. Lack of participation on the children's part might indicate that the material is too difficult. Rhythm instruments and a marching band are a fun activity, and they also provide variety.

Listening to records can be an active or passive musical activity. Both are positive forms. Active listening can introduce the children to a new experience: marching around the room on tiptoes or heels, galloping like horses, or swimming like fish. A whole group of children can be trees swaying in the wind, flowers reaching for the sun, or creatures crouching under a rock in a rainstorm. Passive listening to records or a soft musical instrument like a guitar is calming and may serve for a few minutes as an alternative to a nap, which frequently becomes a battleground. Children can put their heads on their folded hands and relax after a strenuous outdoor playtime. Instrumental pieces provide a nice contrast to the popular music that is more frequently heard.

CREATIVE ACTIVITIES

Blocks

Blocks have a versatility that allows them to play a role in many of the activities previously discussed. Most of all, they are greatly loved by children of all ages.

Blocks are loved by very young children who use them with delight for one of their first play experiences. If they are soft and foamy, they might chew on them and squeeze them until they discover that blocks can be stacked and turned and rolled. Building a tower of even two blocks is an achievement for a one-year-old child! They look at it in amazement and, with only a little encouragement, their towers will grow higher and higher. And this is only the beginning of most children's love affair with blocks. The toddler discovers that they are unbreakable and one can do many different things with them—fit them together, pull them apart, study their shapes—providing endless hours of fun and incidental learning. Blocks stay with children all through their growing years. Experimentation becomes fancier, buildings more complicated, but the delight remains. Blocks are also a wonderful teaching tool. They can be used to clarify number concepts, shapes, length and width, and even more complicated concepts like balance and stability. They strengthen eye-hand coordination and small motor control.

They come in many shapes, forms, and sizes, in many materials, and many colors. Whether they are made of wood, cardboard, foam, or heavy plastic, they invite experimentation on all age levels. Imaginative play with blocks is limitless and success is assured. Blocks permit individual ingenuity and their lack of structure makes them failure proof. Children can use them to express concerns about themselves, building only tiny structures away from the other children, or not using them at all, showing their fearfulness of failure. Blocks are also a wonderful socializing tool. Children play with them in groups and learn the fun of creating something together, the give-and-take of a joint project. Of all toys, blocks are tops!

Being creative is an attitude; it is not dependent on training. Some people can use pipe cleaners, egg cartons, corks, or strawberry containers to create. Others need more formal materials like paint, clay, playdough, and water. Their communality is the fact that they permit the children nonverbal, unhampered opportunities to express feelings in their very own ways. Creativity presupposes an adult whose attitude is uncritical, encouraging, nonspecific, and accepting.

Most small children paint spontaneously without worrying whether or not they have artistic talent. Somehow this is suppressed during the growing-up process. Maybe the trees painted do not look like trees, or the pumpkin is purple; but what matters is the child's enjoyment and the adult's acceptance of the child's individuality. The following poem is a good example of a child's sad but not unusual experience.

The Little Boy

Once a little boy went to school.
He was quite a little boy.
And it was quite a big school.
But when the little boy
Found that he could go to his room
By walking right in from the door outside,
He was happy.
And the school did not seem
Quite so big any more.

One morning,
When the little boy had been in school awhile,
The teacher said:
"Today we are going to make a picture."
"Good," thought the little boy.
He liked to make pictures.
He could make all kinds:
Lions and tigers,
Chickens and cows,
Trains and boats—
And he took out his box of crayons
And began to draw.

But the teacher said: "Wait!
It is not time to begin!"
And she waited until everyone looked ready.

"Now," said the teacher,
"We are going to make flowers."
"Good!" thought the little boy.
He liked to make flowers,
And he began to make beautiful ones
With his pink and orange and blue crayons.

But the teacher said, "Wait!
And I will show you how."
And she drew a flower on the blackboard.
It was red, with a green stem.
"There," said the teacher.
"Now you may begin."

The little boy looked at the teacher's flower.
Then he looked at his flower.
He liked his flower better than the teacher's

But he did not say this.
He just turned his paper over,
And made a flower like the teacher's.
It was red, with a green stem.

On another day,
When the little boy had opened
The door from the outside all by himself,
The teacher said,
"Today we are going to make something with clay."
"Good!" thought the little boy.
He liked clay.
He could make all kinds of things with clay:
Snakes and snowmen,
Elephants and mice,
Cars and trucks—
And he began to pull and pinch
His ball of clay.

But the teacher said,
"Wait! It is not time to begin!"
And she waited until everyone looked ready.

"Now," said the teacher,
"We are going to make a dish."
"Good!" thought the little boy.
He liked to make dishes,
And he began to make some
That were all shapes and sizes.

But the teacher said, "Wait!
And I will show you how."
And she showed everyone how to make
One deep dish.
"There," said the teacher.
"Now you may begin."

The little boy looked at the teacher's dish.
Then he looked at his own.
He liked his dishes better than the teacher's
But he did not say this.
He just rolled his clay into a big ball again
And made a dish like the teacher's.
It was a deep dish.

And pretty soon
The little boy learned to wait,
And to watch,
And to make things just like the teacher.
And pretty soon

He didn't make things of his own anymore.

Then it happened
That the little boy and his family
Moved to another house,
In another city,
And the little boy
Had to go to another school.

This school was even Bigger
Than the other one,
And there was not a door from the outside
Into his room.
He had to go up some big steps,
And walk down a long hall
To get to his room.

And the very first day
He was there,
The teacher said,
"Today we are going to make a picture."
"Good!" thought the little boy,
And he waited for the teacher
To tell him what to do.
But the teacher didn't say anything.
She just walked around the room.

When she came to the little boy
She said, "Don't you want to make a picture?"
"Yes," said the little boy,
"What are we going to make?"
"I don't know until you make it," said the teacher.
"How shall I make it?" said the little boy.
"Why, any way you like," said the teacher.
"And any color?" said the little boy.
"Any color," said the teacher,
"If everyone made the same picture,
And used the same colors,
How would I know who made what,
And which was which?"
"I don't know," said the little boy.
And he began to make pink and orange and blue flowers.

He liked his new school...
Even if it didn't have a door
Right in from the outside!

Helen E. Buckley

Painting

For young children, easel painting with broad, short-handled brushes and bright colors is most satisfactory, particularly if good, large-sized paper is used. It is fun to watch the intense expression on children's faces, their astonishment and pleasure at a creation. You can admire the colors used, the space filled or left empty, the thickness of the paint, or the dots and lines. Nothing kills the spirit faster than the question, "What is it?" The child will either become angry, cover the whole page with paint (often black), tear it up, or quickly go on to another activity. Children need enough space around the easel to step back and admire their work, for an adult to go by, and maybe for another child to run past. Tidiness and cleanliness are undoubtedly next to godliness, but not while painting. Having a washcloth next to the easel would have discouraged even Picasso! Putting aprons or big shirts on the children and rolling up their sleeves can enhance their creativity.

Paint boxes and water colors demand entirely different abilities than easel painting. They demand more control, are less relaxing, and are harder for two- and three-year-olds. The colors are likely to become messed up, the paper to tear, and the activity to last only a few minutes. Finger paints can be saved for later; or if some children are ready while others are not, the latter group can be given tongue depressors or spoons to use instead of their fingers. Joining the fun yourself will convince the children that there is nothing to be afraid of. Extra hands can be essential when finger painting—it does easily "get out of hand," and painted faces, arms, and hair might not be appreciated by parents. It is a fun activity, and with planning, the number of variations are endless: String or sponges can be used instead of brushes, material instead of paper; but chocolate pudding should not be substituted for brown paint! Food is to eat, and paint is to paint.

There are countless interpretations of children's paintings. For example, what colors are used? Checking that a variety is available should precede your diagnosing depression because of black paint or aggression because of red paint! Are there layers of overpaint? Does the child paint the same design over and over? Are the child's motions rhythmical? Is the brush used as a weapon, the paint thrown on the paper?

Water

And then there is water! This is another favorite activity of young children that serves many purposes: It is failure proof, it is relaxing, and it can mark a social occasion. Although friendships are not struck at the well any more, many friendships are started at the water table.

The children blow bubbles, learn to pour, bathe their babies, give shampoos, splash, and share containers, cups, and almost anything. But water play can also be educational: What floats? What sinks? What happens when water freezes, when it boils? What happens when a baster is used, a funnel, a pitcher, a straw? Very few children are afraid of water play; for many it is an introduction to being freer and happier. Sleeves do need to be rolled up and aprons put on. Some children refuse the aprons in the beginning but learn quickly that being wet is not much fun. Natural consequences might be the best teacher, for getting into an argument will ruin the activity for the child (Mills, 1990).

Clay and Playdough

Clay and playdough serve several purposes. Playdough is probably easier for very young children to use than the more difficult to manipulate clay. The children can manufacture it themselves and add color. It keeps in working condition longer, as it consists of flour, water, salt, and a little oil, and it is inexpensive and safe. Adding a little food coloring to "cookie dough" can teach that purple cookies are acceptable and fun.

Working with playdough and/or clay is a creative activity only if creativity is permitted. No specific object needs to be made. On the contrary, the pleasure lies in the plasticity, the easy changeability, the destruction, and the renewal. Nothing has to be perfect, and no model has to be followed. Playdough lends itself to the creation of cookies and hamburgers, which can then lead to a tea or dinner party, as well as to making an elephant or a snowman. Some children will just roll and cut with a cookie cutter, while others are intent on creating recognizable objects. It is helpful not to interpret the children's finished products. Not every snake or elephant trunk is a phallic symbol! Care needs to be taken not to model for the children—it easily creates frustration if the therapist's product is perfect and theirs is not. Many children cannot or will not hold a pencil, but they will gladly manipulate, roll, and handle clay. These activities improve small-motor coordination and will in time lead to the use of pencils and crayons.

Clay and playdough can be a substitute for hitting peers and are a more acceptable way of getting rid of negative feelings. A rubber or plastic hammer with a glob of clay works well to show feelings without the need to verbalize, explain, or pinpoint the source of anger or frustration. A tree stump and nails are great for older children for the same reason—regular hammers are recommended: The children manage well and take it as a sign of your confidence in them. Woodworking for boys *and* girls can be a creative activity, a small-motor activity, and pure fun, helping to delay gratification and lengthen attention span. Making an airplane one day and painting it the next might be a totally new learning experience.

Puppets play an important role in group activities. They should be used as a group activity rather than in free play, since they frequently overstimulate children unless the activity is carefully directed. Puppets of all kinds might be used, but those representing people are most helpful. Social interactions ranging from sharing, making friends, and playing with different people to trying a new activity can be acted out, first by the teacher using each hand for a puppet and then with one or two children. Puppetry provides visual as well as auditory stimuli, and children usually love it. Puppets should be realistic and well made.

SNACK OR LUNCH

The Center provides snacks not only to feed hungry children who need some healthy food but also to observe their behavior during an activity that frequently causes trouble at home and to assess their self-care skills. New and different foods also stimulate talk about different cultures. Observations can be made of hoarding behaviors, seating arrangements, and the child's ability to wait, to take turns, to ask for another cracker, or to participate in conversation.

Mary, age 4, grabbed all the crackers she could reach during snack and crumbled them up in a pile in front of her before eating them. She thus assured herself of her share without interference from any other child or adult. It took time to make up for years of unfulfilled promises to establish trust that she would get her share.

Frequently, children prepare their own snack; they love to make pancakes, Jell-O, stone soup, green scrambled eggs (together with Dr. Seuss), french toast, puddings, and other delicacies. Snack is a lighthearted time that can also serve to diffuse a troubled morning or afternoon. After all, food in our society means love, and children and adults interpret it as such. Hot chocolate is a great tranquilizer for children and adults alike. Parents observing the group through the one-way window are often astonished at their children's willingness at the Center to eat foods they would not touch at home.

Parents are expected to provide a sack lunch. However, some children regularly come without lunch, an indication of the parent's lack of understanding of the child's needs. This gives the parent therapists an idea that maybe providing lunch needs to be the treatment goal for these parents. All children who come without lunch are given something to tide them over.

Lunch is often more difficult; it comes either at the end of a busy morning, when children are becoming tired, or at the beginning of an afternoon, after a long bus ride. Physical space seems particularly important at lunch time. Placemats delineate space and might prevent trouble.

As noted at the beginning of this chapter, programming activities in a child-oriented setting is a means to an end, not an end in itself. To what Mary McCracken (1975) said in her touching book *A Circle of Children*—namely, that one needs "a listening heart and a strong back" (p. 12) to work with children with emotional problems or other disabilities—I would add that one also needs a sense of humor and deep commitment.

Understanding how each child reacts to an activity, to another child, to an adult, and how it can be recorded to make others see the whole child is the aim of the next chapter.

Chapter 8
Observations and Report Writing

INTRODUCTION

Observations are basic in the understanding of children—whether at home, in school, or in a therapeutic situation. Observations, which are the basis for report writing, follow the preschool child like a life script and influence placement in special classes as well as the teacher's expectations. Knowing that the child needs time to warm up to people, to a new situation, or to a task will help the teacher in planning. A child with a low frustration tolerance to failure, information learned from a report based on observation in preschool, can be given short assignments.

Observing a child, particularly in a group situation, is a skill that needs to be practiced. Though a stop watch and a rating scale are useful tools, even more important is the ability of observers to involve all their senses in the process. A "potted palm" role of total passivity is not recommended. "The process of observing is a very active one, calling for as much concentration, empathy and sensitivity to behavior cues as you can muster" (Carbonara, 1961, p. 2). A visual memory helps greatly and can be developed. Until that happens, a small sketch of the children's positions is of help.

It is better for an observer to sit rather than stand and to maintain some distance from the child or the group of children to be observed. Observers need to stay out of the way of teachers, therapists, or child-care workers, remembering that the children are their major responsibility. It is helpful for the observer to know what to look for: Are data needed to better understand the child's social interaction or length of attention span during certain activities? Is acceptance of routines the question? Observation is like gathering evidence for a legal presentation that involves no hearsay, no interpretation, no projection of one's own feelings, just clear perceptions of the happening. Observations of different areas, like behavior toward peers or adults, use of materials, tempo of body movements, and special mannerisms, result in an overall picture of the child. A summary report, a written script accompanying children out of preschool into kindergarten or out of kindergarten into first grade, will contain interpretations of behavior based on reality that will be useful for the future.

GENERAL GUIDELINES

Observations must be immediate, objective, and specific. *Immediate* observation is only possible in a group situation if a special observer is assigned to the group, either a volunteer, a practicum student, or an aide who has received special training in observing and recording. A general statement about the group atmosphere should be included. It is important to discover the antecedents of the child's best behavior and drop the habit of observing only pathology or negative behaviors. Making use of the child's "being good" might help to create situations and programs built on observed strength leading to behavioral changes.

Objective means noninterpretive, which means writing it as you see it: what the child is doing, not why the child is doing it. For instance, "Johnny did not tie his shoes," rather than "Johnny could not tie his shoes" or "Johnny did not want to tie his shoes" or "Johnny was angry, and that's why he did not tie his shoes" or "Johnny wanted me to tie his shoes, which is why he did not do it." Though each of these statements is possibly accurate, it becomes an interpretation rather than an observation and, thus, it becomes a nonobjective statement.

Specific means zeroing in on only one activity or issue. It is better to say, "Mary approached the table prepared with paper and scissors. She picked up the scissors with her left hand in the palmer grip. No cutting resulted. She dropped the scissors and left the activity." This is preferable to "Mary is left-handed and cannot cut. She has low frustration tolerance and does not complete activities." The temptation is great to make generalizations that might or might not be applicable. Mary might not be totally left-handed, and her frustration level may be age-appropriate for other activities, which she then completes.

In the area of self-care skills, an *appropriate* observation would be the following: Tim would not enter the bathroom. He wet shortly after and changed himself. He finished his food quickly and asked for more. Tim put on his snowsuit and asked for help with his boots. He did not wear a hat. An *inappropriate* observation might read: Tim refused to use the bathroom; he is not toilet trained but wets. He ate a lot and always wanted more. He wanted attention by not putting on his boots and a hat.

An *appropriate* observation during storytime might read: Leslie laughed for ten seconds during a funny story. This was the first time a positive affect was noted. The other children joined in, and she smiled. An *inappropriate* observation of the same behavior might read: Leslie laughed hysterically and disturbed storytime for everybody. She was removed to time-out.

The following table may help to sharpen observational skills.

Table 8.1
Observational Skills

Name Date	C	S	R	N
C=Consistently, S=Sometimes, R=Rarely, N=Never	C	S	R	N
INITIAL IMPRESSION				
SIZE: (Circle) Average				
Tall				
Small				
Obese				
Other:				
FACIAL EXPRESSION: Eager				
Friendly				
Anxious				
Pouty				
Angry				
Other:				
POSTURE: Slouchy				
Straight				
Other:				
APPROACH: Quick				
Hesitant				
Eager				
Anxious				
Refuses				
Runs in room				
Won't come in				
Wants hug				
Other:				

Table 8.1 (continued)

C=Consistently, S=Sometimes, R=Rarely, N=Never	C	S	R	N
SELF-CARE: TOILETING				
Toilets independently				
Going frequently				
Wetting				
Soiling				
Crying when diapered				
Crying when asked to go				
Other:				
SELF-CARE: EATING				
Hoarding food				
Asking for more				
Sharing				
Keeping food in mouth				
Gagging				
Refusing to eat				
Other:				
SELF-CARE: DRESSING				
Puts on snowsuit				
Puts on boots				
Puts on swimsuit				
Buttons				
Zips				
Snaps				
Tries to put on snowsuit				
Tries to put on boots				
Tries to put on swimsuit				
Tries to button				
Tries to zip				
Tries to snap				
Other:				
SMALL MOTOR SKILLS				
Holds scissors				
Cuts: Right hand				
Left hand				

Table 8.1 (continued)

C=Consistently, S=Sometimes, R=Rarely, N=Never	C	S	R	N
Holds pencil: Palmer grip				
Pincer grip				
Scribbles				
Paints				
Uses clay				
Other:				
LARGE MOTOR SKILLS				
Walks on tiptoes				
Runs				
Stumbles				
Falls				
Pedals a trike				
Throws a ball				
Uses a slide				
Climbs on bars				
Isolated outside				
Ascends stairs				
Descends stairs				
Other:				
MOVEMENT				
Participates				
Hesitant				
Refuses				
Other:				
GROUP ACTIVITIES				
STORY TIME: Listen: 5 / 10 minutes				
Participates				
Joins group				
Is disruptive				
Joins disruption				
Other:				
ART: Participates				
Paints the same direction				
Uses same color (which color)				
Hesitant to do something new				
Likes art work				

Table 8.1 (continued)

C=Consistently, S=Sometimes, R=Rarely, N=Never	C	S	R	N
Takes it home				
Tears it up				
Needs models				
Is imaginative				
Fearful of fingerpaints				
Other:				
PLAY: Solitary				
Interactive				
Cooperative				
Parallel				
The same toy				
The same child				
Shares				
Asks for help				
Has fun				
Plays aggressively				
Free play				
Does not know what to do				
Uses toy idiosyncratically (how)				
Attention span: 5 minutes				
1 minute				
Stuck				
Other:				
LANGUAGE: Speaks clearly				
Words (how many)				
Sentences				
Sound substitutions (which sounds)				
Repeats words				
Names gender correctly				
Voice volume: Loud				
Whispers				
Swearing				
Toilet talk				
Baby talk				

Table 8.1 (continued)

C=Consistently, S=Sometimes, R=Rarely, N=Never	C	S	R	N
Spontaneous speech				
Mute				
Speaks rarely				
Speaks to peers only				
Whiny				
Other:				
COGNITIVE SKILLS				
Can count				
Tells colors				
Knows function of objects				
Classify by sight				
Classify by sound				
Classify by smell				
Match colors				
Match shapes				
Can copy designs				
Sequence				
Other:				
INTERACTIONS				
WITH PEERS: Reaches out - Same sex				
Biggest				
Smallest				
Responds - Verbally				
Positively				
Negatively				
Defends				
Other:				
WITH ADULTS: Responsive to outreach-Physical				
Responsive to outreach-Verbal				
Eye contact				
Argumentative				
Asks for a hug				
Withdraws from touch				
Other:				

Table 8.1 (continued)

C=Consistently, S=Sometimes, R=Rarely, N=Never	C	S	R	N
AFFECT				
Generally appropriate				
Intense				
Silly				
Sad				
Angry				
Happy				
Withdrawn				
Lonely				
Quiet				
Boisterous				
Other:				
COPING WITH CRISIS				
Asks for help				
Aggressive (how)				
Can solve verbally				
Can process				
Finds alternative solutions				
Expects adults to solve				
Other:				

An example of an *appropriate, objective, and specific* observation for an initial impression is the following: Ann (age three) is a small, dark-complected child with large brown eyes. She is of average build for her age. She hid in back of her mother, but smiled. Ann did not shake hands, but quickly entered the playroom. She cried for five minutes when her mother left; then Ann joined the children at the water table. An *inappropriate* observation would be this: Ann is a very pretty, small black child. She was anxious and looked for protection from her mother. She was unfriendly and babyish. Ann finally played with the children at the water table.

REPORT WRITING

Observations form the basis for parent-teacher conferences, report writing, and planning for the use of intervention strategies. The richness and precision of the language, rather than just a list of traits, result in a vivid picture of the child. A lack of precision in everyday conversations makes observations and report writing particularly difficult. In verbal interchange we also use gestures, facial expression, and body language; but in a report, language is the only means of interchange.

Professionals are responsible for describing children in a way most helpful for their future, be that school placement or special treatment.

The use of words is just like the use of tools: It has to be learned and then practiced in order to best express what needs to be said. Many behavior checklists are available, but a list frequently needs to be amplified when one deals with preschool children. Some school districts classify behavior-disordered children into two groups, "externalizers and internalizers" (Kukic and Reavis, 1991, p. 9), which corresponds to the mental health classifications of noncompliant, acting-out, oppositional children in contrast to withdrawn, depressed, anxious, dysthymic children. Specific checklists and comparative data are suggested for use with nonreferred children to avoid possible legal repercussions of placement. In therapeutic preschools or day-treatment centers where the children are prescreened, such caution is not deemed necessary. Observations need to be objective, however; and within a formal setting, greater emphasis must be placed on developmental appropriateness, affect, and relationships rather than on cognitive functioning. As pointed out earlier, psychological jargon and general statements should be avoided in observation reporting. With greater cooperation between educators and mental health professionals, as discussed by William Morse (1992), greater emphasis on the pupil's emotional needs may be an achievable goal. One school district in Ogden, Utah, is pioneering such a model (Freston, 1992).

Observation of the child's behavior in group forms the basis for report writing and, at times, greatly influences the child's future in school and at home. The following reports have traveled across the country to George's new school and therapist (see Appendix F).

THE CHILDREN'S CENTER INITIAL REPORT

NAME: George   DATE: June 87
DOB: 3/84   THERAPISTS:
AGE: 3–4   SUPERVISOR:
ADMISSION: 6/87

Data

George was referred to The Children's Center by his foster mother. Referral concerns include sleep disturbance, night terrors, and aggressive behavior with siblings and natural children of foster parents. George is the second child of a family of seven children who are currently placed in a foster home. The natural parents' whereabouts are unknown at the present time. George was admitted to a morning activity group in June 1987.

Behavioral Review

George came to The Children's Center on his first day with his foster mother and the parent worker. George had a difficult time separating from his foster mother. When it was time for her to leave, George started crying and went into the hall as if to follow her, but he was helped back into the room by a therapist. George was able to stop crying rather quickly. When a therapist invited him to engage in the activity in progress, he responded by asking if he could draw. George kept his lunch box next to him for the first twenty minutes of the day, then allowed a child to put it away. George stayed on the periphery for most of the day.

Self-Care Skills

George's self-care skills appear to be age-appropriate. He is able to eat independently and does so while maintaining a neat appearance. George is able to toilet, as well as to wash and dry his hands independently.

Speech/Affect

George's speech is below age-appropriate norms. He is easy to understand, but he speaks in a soft monotone. He speaks so quietly that he must frequently repeat what he said. George's affect is flat. He has very little facial expression. George smiles so very tentatively that it is not clear if he is smiling.

Small- and Large-Motor Skills

George's small-and large-motor skills are age-appropriate. He is right-handed and holds a pencil with a pincer grasp. George is able to cut with direction and force. He can run, climb, and ride a tricycle.

Interaction with Peers

George makes and accepts minimal outreach with peers. Most of his outreach comes during lunch time, when he asks the children to share their food. When children invite him to play, he accepts their invitation only if accompanied by an adult. George is an extremely isolated child. He has minimal defense skills. During conflict, he gives up quickly even when supported by an adult.

Interaction with Adults

George is closer to adults than to peers. He is dependent on adults and stays near their side for the majority of the day. George will invite adults to play and will ask them to come along when he is invited by another child. If the adult cannot go, he will not go, either. George appears fearful of asking questions. He will ask in a soft, shaky voice and with downcast eyes. George is able to respond to adults' requests.

Strengths

George is a cute, dark-haired, blue-eyed boy. He has well-developed small-and large-motor skills and is capable of successfully completing projects. George shows affection toward adults by hugging, holding hands, and asking to be held. He responds to adults' requests appropriately. George is easy to get along with and is fun to be with.

Initial Speech and Language Report

George was given a speech and language assessment because of limited participation in group speech. He came willingly and immediately started asking questions about what he could play with. His sentences were three to seven words in length with good syntax. His semantics and pragmatics were adequate for his age. An articulation test indicated that George has acquired his sounds to an age-appropriate level. He produces the 'L' and 'Th' phonemes in words, and the 'sh,' 'ch,' 'zh,' 'dz,' and 'R' are developing. George will continue in group speech weekly to encourage verbal participation, but no further speech reevaluations are recommended.

Recommendations and Exit Data

It is recommended that George remain in day treatment at The Children's Center until the following goals have been achieved unless new areas of concern arise.

Goal 1: Engage in parallel play away from the adults for a minimum of ten minutes three times daily.

Goal 2: Responds verbally to conversations directed toward him once per activity.

Therapist   Assistant Therapist   Supervisor

It is important to give enough detail to make the child come alive for the reader without becoming repetitive and having to write a novella;

on the other hand, bare-facts reporting will miss the child's strengths and weaknesses. A sample report follows.

THE CHILDREN'S CENTER 90-DAY TREATMENT PLAN REVIEW

DOB: 3/84   DATE: September 1987
AGE: 3–7   THERAPIST:
SUPERVISOR:

Data

No major changes have occurred in George's home since the last reporting period.

Behavioral Observations

George is timid when he arrives at the Center, but as the day progresses, he becomes more assertive and will tell adults and peers what he wants. He will say assertively, "Pass the milk" or "I want a Skittle."

He continues to attach quickly to the adult volunteers, and he tries to manipulate the adults to do things for him by refusing to do things on his own or acting helpless. He will say, "You do it" or "I can't do it." Once he was cold and wanted a sweater. When he was encouraged to select one on his own, he refused.

He continues to improve in the area of interactive play. He will accept outreach from peers with little or no encouragement from adults. He will not initiate interactive play with peers. He appears to have a low self-esteem and will always give in to peers' demands.

George will comply with adult requests. His compliance is sometimes slow, and it could be that he is seeking attention from the adults. George expresses little desire for art or dance activities; but when he does join in, he enjoys himself.

He plays with his peers and never creates tension during play. He is showing more facial expression and will cheerfully smile on occasion. His self-care and motor skills continue to be age-appropriate.

Progress toward Goals

Goal 1: George is now able to play parallel for one to two minutes three times daily independent of adult with primary and social reinforcement.

Goal 2: George responds verbally to conversation directed toward him once per activity (goal achieved).

Goal 3: Responds to foster parents' directives approximately 50 percent of the time.

New Areas of Concern

When George comes to group, it appears that he has been crying. His eyes are often puffy and swollen.

Results of Discontinuing Treatment

Discontinuing treatment could result in deterioration of George's self-esteem and his interactive skills with peers and adults.

THE CHILDREN'S CENTER 90-DAY TREATMENT PLAN REVIEW

DOB: 3/84   DATE: December 1987
AGE: 3–10   THERAPIST:
                    SUPERVISOR:

Data

George's group has had several children leave and new children enter during the past three months. Reports from foster parents indicate that his natural father was murdered in December.

Behavioral Observations

George is demonstrating more self-confidence, makes more outreach to adults, and is not nearly as helpless or isolated as he was at admission. George seems to be very concerned about food, and he is always asking, "When are we going to have snack?" or "When are we going to have lunch?" He comes to group saying he is hungry. The therapists offer him crackers, and he will eat his share and then ask for more. Sometimes George will become upset with an adult when he is told that he will need to wait for snack. He will say things such as "You're stupid" or "Dummy."

George will inappropriately seek adult attention. He will often talk to adults when an adult is talking. When the adult explains that it is his or her turn to talk, George becomes angry and will kick the adult. From this point forward, the behavior escalates, and George will begin tantruming and can become destructive. He will kick, throw chairs, and tear up paper. It appears he is seeking attention and a need has been overlooked. Sometimes he will throw a tantrum if he is forced to go outside. If he is left alone to decide, he will eventually join the group outside. During outside time, George usually rides bikes and plays near an adult.

George will play parallel with his peers, but rarely will he say a complete sentence to a peer. He is not assertive in expressing his disappointment when a peer takes his toy away.

George has come to the Center with his pants on backwards. He enjoys cutting paper into little pieces, even if the art project requires a large shape. George is usually able to remain at the circle and carry out his helping jobs responsively. He has begun to participate in group dance activities he would not do before.

Progress toward Goals

Goal 1: George is isolative, and limited progress has been made in parallel play. The goal was discontinued and a more appropriate goal was set.

Goal 3: Foster mother has infrequent contact with The Children's Center. Little progress made on goal.

Goal 4: George will carry on five-minutes conversations. George is now able to make one or two sentences.

Goal 5: George will assert wants and needs once per activity. George still needs help when he is frustrated with his peers. He is making positive self-statements during the day.

Goal 6: George will accept positive comments. George is accepting physical outreach and positive comments better, but he will still react negatively or seem embarrassed.

Continuing Need for Treatment and New Areas of Concern

George showed almost no reaction to deaths of his father and mother and has not discussed them in group.

Results of Discontinuing Treatment

Discontinuing treatment could result in deterioration of George's social skills with peers and adults.

THE CHILDREN'S CENTER 90-DAY TREATMENT PLAN REVIEW

DOB: 3/84   DATE: March 1988
AGE: 4–1   THERAPIST:
            SUPERVISOR:

Data

During this reporting period, George and his foster family moved. George has begun individual therapy two times per week with a female therapist, effective January 1988. There have also been changes in the group makeup; however, George has appeared unaffected by these changes. In December his biological father died, but George has made few comments regarding his father's death.

Behavioral Observations

Due to George's increased anxiety over food, the daily schedule has been altered in order to accommodate some of his needs. Each day the children have snack upon their arrival. George is eager to begin eating and appears quite hungry, for he eats constantly for fifteen to twenty minutes, if allowed to do so. Throughout snack he asked for more food and milk to drink. Therapists give him an appropriate amount in small portions when he asks. When asked to clean up, he begins to stuff the remainder of his snack into his moth. After eating his stomach is usually quite distended.

Lunchtime has become a difficult time for George. Previously, his lunch of a whole sandwich, fruit, and treat was appealing to him. His lunch has recently consisted of half a sandwich and broken potato chips. George becomes easily frustrated, sometimes throwing his sandwich, yelling, "I don't like that kind!" When therapists offer their help, he puts his head down on the table and pouts. George prolongs the process of verbalizing and attempting to resolve the problem. He uses a demanding tone of voice and refuses to accept the alternative presented to him. On one occasion, George worked on resolving the problem by finding a peer who was willing to trade sandwiches. By the smile on his face, George appeared pleased with himself.

George continues to have trouble defending himself. When a peer grabs a toy from him, he is not able to verbalize his feelings nor does he attempt to retrieve the toy. After these incidents George usually pouts, lies down on the floor, and pushes away anyone who attempts to help him. After a few minutes, he is able to accept comfort from an adult, but only when the adult has reached out to him. It takes several minutes of sitting on an adult's lap before he is confident in rejoining the group. The initial conflict is rarely resolved, and it is difficult because he ignores you.

George very much enjoys the time he spends with adults. He frequently asks to be held and carried, and he can sometimes ask an adult for this. George has failed to develop any relationships with his peers. He is able to play parallel with them and is watchful of them, but he does not initiate activity or seem to have interest in interacting with them. George also does not seem to gain much enjoyment from any particular type of toy or activity.

It has been observed that George's main focus during his time at The Children's Center revolves around satisfying his neverending need for food and physical closeness from an adult.

Progress toward Goals

Goal 5: Assert wants or needs verbally. George yells and throws tantrums in order to get his needs met. However, he is progressing in this area. He had been very passive and unassertive in the past.

Goal 6: Will accept a positive comment from adults. George can tolerate a minimal amount of affectionate outreach from adults at this time. He is progressing in this area, accepting praise occasionally. His self-image remains poor, so that he disbelieves most positive comments.

Goal 3 COLLATERAL: George will respond to foster parents' directives 75 percent of the time. Foster parents express frustration at George's neediness. Apparently they are pursuing adoption of all (seven) of George's siblings now in their home. Progress toward goal minimal.

New Areas of Concern

See report above.

Results of Discontinuing Treatment

George needs continued treatment if he is to be successfully adopted.

Supervisor's Comments

George is a very disturbed child who is demonstrating regressive behavior, such as overeating and hoarding, as he tries to cope with the loss of his father and mother and the loss of individual adult attention in his life. Individual therapy should help provide some support for this troubled child.

THE CHILDREN'S CENTER DISCHARGE SUMMARY

DOB: 3/84   ADMIT DATE: June 1987
AGE: 4–7   DISCHARGE DATE: October 1988
        THERAPIST:
        ASSISTANT THERAPIST:
        SUPERVISOR:

Presenting Complaint

George was referred to The Children's Center by his foster mother. Referral concerns include sleep disturbance, night terrors, and aggressive behavior with siblings.

Reason for Discharge

Adopted out of state.

Summary of Service

Child

George entered an activity therapy group in June 1987. He transferred to a higher-functioning group in April 1988. He discharged in October 1988.

Parent

The foster parents came in regularly for assistance in managing George and his sister, who was also in treatment at The Children's Center.

Treatment Review Achievement of Goals

Child

When George first entered The Children's Center in June 1987, his affect was flat. George smiled so tentatively that therapists were unsure if it was a smile at all. His speech was below age-appropriate norms. Although he was easy to understand and his semantics and pragmatics were adequate for his age, George spoke in a monotone that was so soft he was frequently asked to repeat what he said.

George made minimal outreach to peers. He was an extremely isolated child who accepted another child's invitation to play only if accompanied by an adult. He was closer to adults than peers, and very dependent on therapists.

In September 1987 George was still timid but a bit more assertive when expressing a need or want. He began to smile more and show more facial expression. He was also able to accept outreach from peers with little or no encouragement from adults, but he would not initiate play. He appeared to have a low self-esteem and always gave in to peer's demands. George frequently acted helpless in order to manipulate adults, and he was slow to comply.

By December 1987 George demonstrated more self-confidence and made more outreach to adults. He was not nearly as helpless or isolated as he had been at admission. George became very concerned with food and came to group saying he was hungry. When therapists explained he must wait for snack, he responded by telling them to "shut up" and calling them a name.

George also began seeking adult attention inappropriately. He often became angry with adults when they told him it was their turn to talk. He reacted to this by kicking, tantruming, and becoming destructive. When George was left alone, he usually rejoined the group on his own.

In March 1988 George was extremely obsessed with food. Therapists even altered the daily schedule so that he could eat a snack upon his arrival. George continued to have trouble defending himself. When a conflict arose between George and a peer, he would not verbalize his feelings or attempt to resolve the problem. After these incidents, he usually pouted, lay on the floor, and pushed away anyone who attempted to comfort him.

George loves to spend time with adults. He frequently asks to be held and carried. He has failed to develop any relationships with his peers. It was observed that George's main focus during his time at The Children's Center revolved around satisfying his neverending need for food and physical closeness with an adult. Attendance was sporadic during this reporting period, and no excuses were given for his absences. He came to The Children's Center wearing his pants backward; he was dirty, had uncut hair, and was always hungry.

In June 1988 George's mood swings became more prominent, becoming alternately depressed and very needy for attention to extremely silly. He came with signs of physical abuse, a hand imprint on the side of his face. George did, however, start talking more and asserting himself with the therapists to get his needs met.

By August 1988 George was interacting more spontaneously with better affect. He joined the group more often on his own. However, he became extremely silly and was easily overstimulated. He can be very noncompliant, but he responded well to positive primary reinforcers. He still was eating large amounts of food, but he was not dawdling as much over snack and lunch.

When George was given a compliment, he often became silly, blinking eyes, squinting, and covering his ears. He seemed genuinely happy to be at The Children's Center, as evident in his greetings to therapists.

In September and October, prior to his discharge, George became friendly with a particular peer in the group. He loved to play hide and seek with this peer and one or two therapists. He was able to engage in limited conversation with this peer and defend himself verbally with all peers in the group. Although George remained overpreoccupied with food, this obsession somewhat diminished.

George often engaged a peer in inappropriate activities to get a reaction from therapists. When George was taken out of the room, he would scream and cry and tell therapists to "shut up." After therapists communicated to George that he could receive attention by asking to go for a walk or to sit in an adult's lap, he was able to calm down and rejoin the group.

A few weeks before George discharged from treatment, he seemed very happy and came to the group with a very bright affect. George enjoyed most activities in group but often said, "Can we skip art?" He enjoyed unstructured play more than before and was able to sustain his play longer.

George still becomes noncompliant and gets intensely angry. He is better able to play interactively with peers, but this skill is very limited and fragile.

George's mood swings are not as pronounced as they were before, and he is able to maintain a medium between depression and silliness for longer periods of time.

About two days before George discharged, he mentioned to the entire group during lunch that he was going with his new mom and dad on a plane. He appeared very happy and excited about this event. However, George told his individual therapist that he hated his new family and did not want to leave The Children's Center.

On George's last day in group, he had numerous conflicts and tore up his graduation crown twice. He was very anxious and clung to adults.

Parent

Very limited progress in goal to help George verbalize his needs. The foster parents' feelings of rejection were paramount, absorbing considerable amounts of their emotional energy. Goal was discontinued upon George's discharge from The Children's Center.

Postdischarge Plan

The adoptive family plans on involving George in family therapy.

Medications

None.

Final Diagnoses

DSM III-R   Diagnosis:

Axis I   Reactive Attachment Disorder of Childhood—313.86

Axis II   None

Axis III   None

Axis IV   4 (stressors)

Axis V   Current GAF: 65. Highest GAF past year: 65

Therapist   Assistant Therapist   Supervisor

The discharge report is usually discussed with the parents at their last session, and behavior rating scales are completed.

George should probably have been placed in the group home rather than in foster care. Prognosis would have been better for adjustment in an adoptive home.

Chapter 9
The Group Home

THE GROUP HOME

Among the world of professionals who provide care to neglected and abused children, there is considerable controversy as to the effectiveness and efficacy of group care for very young children. The Children's Center experience is that some children—even by the age of two—have been so psychologically damaged that life in the intimacy of a "family" setting cannot accommodate their necessary healing. Traditional foster care may, in fact, compound feelings of loss and exacerbate a child's feelings of conflict in loyalty and value between biological and foster parents. These are great emotional demands on a child.

Recent experiences with former clients returning as adults with their own children—some just to say hello and others for help—has strengthened The Children's Center's belief and commitment to residential care for those young children who are in need of substitute care. The Children's Center Group Home has become a touch point of trust for some adults who, as children, were residents.

Suzy M. was adamant with the Department of Social Services that she did not wish her children to experience "foster homes." Her trust was in The Children's Center Group Home. Says Suzy, "I won't be like my mother; I know I need help."

Suzy's four-year-old daughter, Donna, had become totally unmanageable after experiencing abuse from Suzy and Suzy's boyfriend. Donna became a Children's Center resident, and while she learned new skills for relationships and trust, her mother made comparable therapeutic gains. The family was reunited after eight months. Suzy and Donna continue their involvement with The Children's Center, seeking help through family therapy.

The following is an excerpt from a letter sent to me:

Dear Agi,
I hope you remember me. I haven't seen you for about 13 or 14 years. Nancy, my sister, is now married and she has a baby boy about 7 years, 6 months of age. She is doing very well. I am getting married and have no children. I am doing well also.
Please write to me.

Sincerely,
Mary Sue Smith

It was the experience of trust, safety, and hope that brings Suzy M., Mary Sue, and others like them back to The Children's Center. The group home is dedicated to helping children who have been beaten, abandoned, and neglected to regain dignity, build a stronger sense of self, and, most of all, regain trust in themselves and the world.

History

The original group home was established in 1967 as an adjunct to day treatment through a grant from the W. T. Grant Foundation. The main purpose was to provide a viable alternative to the institutionalization of severely disturbed young children. The group home provided twenty-four-hour care, Monday through Friday, for six children ages two to five.

In 1974 the services were expanded to provide twenty-four-hour care for seven children on a seven-day basis.

In 1983 a specially designed home was built and services were extended to include nine children ages two to seven. In addition, children from neighboring states where such services were not available, were accepted for treatment.

Funding

The group home is licensed by the state of Utah through the State Division of Family Services to provide residential services to nine children. Contract services with placement agencies do not fully cover the cost of treatment. The group home relies on foundations, corporations, and private donations to help meet expenses. The Children's Center also contracts with surrounding states that do not have such services available. Arrangements for placement are made through The Children's Center business manager.

Treatment Plan

In addition to the therapy provided by consistent daily living experiences, all children are in individual therapy as well as attend daily activity group therapy sessions at the adjacent day-treatment facility. Speech therapy and individual tutoring is provided to those children requiring it. Parents receive treatment while their child is living in the group home.

Most children placed in the group home have spent their lives in an emotional vacuum—deprived of love, security, and intellectual stimulation. Many symptoms indicate serious emotional disturbance: crying and screaming without apparent reason, violent and self-destructive behavior, withdrawal, not speaking, and lack of concentration.

The goal of this concentrated program is to enhance or create coping strategies in both parents and children and to restore the family situation so the child and family can eventually reunite.

Length of Treatment

Length of treatment in the group home is usually six to nine months. Close cooperation is maintained between the referral agency, the group home supervisor, and the family. Discharge from the group home is a joint decision of all professionals involved, depending on progress of the child, the parent, and the court determination.

Staffing

The group home is staffed by group home parents, day therapists, and weekend counselors. All are trained in the treatment philosophy used at The Children's Center and supervised by an experienced mental health professional. Every effort is made to provide a non-institutional nurturing atmosphere for the children and model for them the functioning of a healthy family system.

Parental Treatment

It is the goal of the group home to try to reunite the family. If this is not possible, The Children's Center works with the referring agency to assist with a child's permanent placement. The Children's Center is not an adoptive agency.

Case Histories

Aaron and Freddie, two brothers, ages 3 and 4, were both silent and withdrawn, made no eye contact, and would lie in a fetal position for hours. They had spent their lives living with their alcohol and drug dependent mother or their elderly grandparents while their mother underwent treatment. Their speech, eating and sleeping patterns were severely delayed relative to peers. The boys' father, also drug dependent, wished to relinquish them to adoptive parents. Their mother did not.

The children were admitted to the group home and began to receive treatment and support. During the next thirteen months, efforts were made (once again) to provide rehabilitation to their mother and reunite the family. The boys established trusting relationships, gained self-confidence, and made rapid progress. However, their mother's progress was not evident. After a lengthy trial, the decision was made to place them in an adoptive home where they live healthy lives and continue to improve.

Chapter 10
Auxiliary Educational Services

INTRODUCTION

In addition to the clinical services discussed extensively in the previous nine chapters, The Children's Center provides auxiliary educational services that form a continuum. They extend the impact of the Center way beyond the families we serve on a daily basis and might well historically be our most significant contribution to the mental health of children. The prevention of serious problems in young children is the most urgent mental health need of our time. The extensive waiting list at The Children's Center indicates the need for it, but its singular uniqueness in the country indicates the difficulties of its financial maintenance. As mentioned in earlier chapters, our waiting lists have increased, the problems of the children referred have become more serious, and the total situation is now more urgent. The auxiliary educational programs are an attempt to provide preventive measures to reduce the need for intensive day-care treatment programs.

Mother-Toddler Program
Kindergarten Outreach Program
Parenting Class
Day-Care Consultation
Training for Graduate Students

THE MOTHER-TODDLER PROGRAM

This program serves children between the ages of eighteen and thirty months. It provides services to families who are concerned about their child's emotional development and/or their mutual relationship. Prior to joining the group, a parent-child meeting is held with the therapist, a developmental history is taken, and, for research purposes, a twenty-five-minute videotaping session is conducted. The time is divided into five minutes of observation of the child's behavior dealing with a frustrating situation (one challenging toy) and the mother's helping style, followed by ten minutes of free play with five or six age-appropriate toys, pick up, and snack. The material is coded and rated according to the mother's sensitivity level and responsiveness.

The groups, consisting of six mother-child dyads, are conducted twice weekly for one and one-half hours for eight weeks at each of the day-treatment centers. Their main aim is to acquaint mothers with developmental expectations, to increase their self-confidence in their parenting skills, and if the need arises, to make an early referral to day treatment. The case history of Ben and his mother can serve as an example.

Ben and his mother were referred to the mother-toddler group by Ben's pediatrician. Ben lived with his mother, father, and infant brother. He was delivered six weeks prematurely and spent the first several weeks of his life in the hospital. His parents spent the first few months of his life uncertain whether he would live. His mother attributed much of their current difficulty to Ben's prematurity and extended hospitalization. At the time of the intake interview, Ben appeared to be experiencing language, social, cognitive, and motor delays.

During the developmental history interview, Ben's mother expressed frustration with the high frequency and intensity of Ben's tantrums. When frustrated, Ben emitted a high-pitched scream that frazzled his mother's nerves. In the presence of a frequent playmate, Ben consistently made attempts to grab the other child's toys. Failure resulted in extended tantrums. Ben's mother also complained that Ben seemed "distant" and "too independent."

In the first few group sessions, Ben threw tantrums very frequently, particularly when unable to attain a desired object. He was aggressive with other children, frequently grabbing their arms, legs, and toys. He moved awkwardly about the room, focusing primarily on toys, showing minimal interest in his mother, peers, or other adults. He generally approached others only for the purpose of attaining a toy in their possession. Ben had difficulty focusing on activities for more than a few minutes. He moved quickly from one toy to the next, and he made repeated attempts to leave the group during snack and circle time.

Ben's mother was initially overwhelmed. She broke into tears on several occasions during the first few sessions, frustrated by her inability to manage Ben's tantrums and aggression. The assurance from other mothers in the group that they often had similar struggles with their children appeared to be very comforting to Ben's mother.

Over the course of the eight weeks, the group focused on several aspects of Ben's and his mother's interactions. First, the group therapist modeled how to redirect Ben to an alternative toy when he attempted to grab toys from others. Ben's mother picked up on this strategy very quickly by watching the group therapist's modeling and by practicing on her own, with feedback from the therapists.

It quickly became apparent that Ben's aggressive behavior was often an effort to initiate an interaction with a peer, rather than a demonstration of frustration or hostility. Pointing this out to his mother allowed her to view his behavior in a much more positive manner. She had been very concerned about her child's "hostility." With group support, she was able to model for Ben more appropriate means of greeting others or initiating an interaction.

Finally, the group focused on increasing the sharing of activities between Ben and his mother. Ben's mother generally jumped into play with Ben, imposing her own agenda on his play activities, attempting to change his ongoing play. Not surprisingly, Ben resisted these attempts, and as a result they spent very little time engaged in shared activities. In order to identify his play agenda, Ben's mother was helped to observe Ben's activity for a few seconds before joining the activity. She could then join his play agenda, participating in his play, rather than making attempts to change it.

By the last two weeks of the group, Ben's tantrums had decreased dramatically. He was beginning to initiate interactions with verbalizations and soft pats on the arm, rather than grabbing and hitting other children to get their attention. Ben was able to focus on activities for longer periods of time, though he still had some difficulty sitting through circle time. Most striking was Ben's increased interest in and interactions with others. He had become a part of the group, seeking interactions and enjoying activities with both adults and peers.

Ben's mother's perception of herself as a parent had improved considerably. By the end of the group, she was able to understand much more of Ben's behavior, was more relaxed in her interactions with him, and was more attuned to his cues and needs than she had been at the beginning. Most importantly, as she reported to a therapist when she left on the last day, she had come to like her child for the first time.

At this time, participation is limited mostly to mothers, since the group meets in the morning. The service, funded by a private foundation, is provided free of charge.

THE KINDERGARTEN OUTREACH PROGRAM

The kindergarten and first grade follow-up program helps children and parents who have attended The Children's Center with the transition into a larger system. The children who need special-class placement are evaluated at The Children's Center, and arrangements are made with the special teaching team for their admission. A mental health professional meets with the parents and the teachers and stays in contact with both throughout the year. Classroom observations and checklists for teachers are used. The Children's Center outreach worker attends staff meetings with the special placement teams in the school districts. The program is also funded by a grant from a private foundation.

THE PARENTING CLASS

The six weekly sessions of the parenting class cover four topics, as listed in the basic guidelines that follow.

Basic Guidelines for Enjoying Your Children

Session I. How a parent influences a child's behavior
    Goals and expectations set by parents

Session II. Self-esteem
    Enhancing self-esteem

Sessions III & IV. Communication
    How to talk so kids will listen and listen so kids will talk

Sessions V & VI. Disciplining the young child
    Purpose of discipline
    Discipline vs. punishment
    Alternatives to punishment
    Natural consequences
    Limits

Discussion and review.

Handouts and several videos are used in all sessions.

DAY-CARE CONSULTATION PROGRAM

With the ever-increasing number of children in daycare, means have to be found to bring mental health principles into their operation. Warehousing thousands of children without meeting their emotional needs will simply not do in the twenty-first century.

The day-care consultation program is an eight-week, on-site program. It comprises three interrelated components: weekly training lectures, hands-on modeling of interventions in groups, and monthly staff training sessions. It is meant to prevent the development of serious problems in the children, to increase the child-care workers' knowledge and confidence levels, and to refer children to special agencies, if needed.

This program is partially funded by the United Way of the Greater Salt Lake Area, the Utah Office of Child Care, and private donations. It is the most economical way to reach large numbers of children and child-care workers.

The program has been expanded to the residents of the House of Hope, a residential facility for chemically addicted women and their children. In addition to on-site visits, psychological evaluations and counseling with mothers are provided. This home is funded and operated by the Utah Alcoholism Foundation, which pays by the hour for the services received.

The Children's Center outreach consultation program could serve as a model and be duplicated in other communities, but only if a day-treatment center is available as backup, not only as a referral source but also as living proof that the advocated strategies and interventions work. Day-treatment centers could also be used as hands-on laboratories for day-care workers, thus offering intensive practical experience.

TRAINING PROGRAM

The Children's Center has provided training for mental health personnel since its inception. Staff members have appointments in the medical school, and in the departments of psychology, social work, and speech pathology at the University of Utah and Brigham Young University; they also supervise students in their respective fields.

The Center offers undergraduate and graduate training for psychologists, social workers, speech pathologists, interns and residents in psychiatry and pediatrics, and psychiatric nurses. Undergraduate students from several universities fulfill practicum requirements at the Center. The interns and residents evaluate children, conduct individual play therapy sessions, and work with parents in counseling and conjoint meetings. They attend weekly seminars, staff meetings, and supervisory sessions.

These auxiliary educational services serve as prevention, as community facilities, and as a continuum of the more intensive clinical services. Although they contribute to the administrative difficulties of the agency, they pay heavy dividends in terms of children's and families' lives.

Chapter 11

Administration

ADMINISTRATION

History of The Children's Center

The Children's Center is a private, nonprofit social agency. The day-treatment program began in 1963, a group home was added in 1967, and a second day-treatment center was opened in 1975 (Plenk, 1986). Though the agency's day-treatment services have not increased, growth of auxiliary clinical and educational services have been considerable. The Center is now providing a continuum of services for young children with behavioral problems. Demands of the multiple, complicated funding sources, as well as the additional services, have necessitated a larger clinical and clerical staff (see Table 11.1).

THE BOARD OF DIRECTORS

The Children's Center Board of Directors has always played a major role in the growth and development of the agency. The enthusiasm of its twenty-four members, combined with their commitment, carried the agency through many crises. The nominating committee carefully considers the age, gender, and professional diversity and expertise of each nominee. In a small private agency, board members must represent the community in order to be effective in advocacy and fund raising. Because fund raising has become progressively more cumbersome, it has developed into the board's major function. The board conducts a highly successful annual fundraiser that has become the main source of income for the endowment fund. Corporations and individuals

Table 11.1
The Children's Center

THE CHILDREN'S CENTER

BOARD OF TRUSTEES   RESEARCH ADVISORY BOARD

EXECUTIVE/MEDICAL DIRECTOR

CLINICAL DIRECTORS	COORDINATORS	RESEARCH DIRECTOR	ADMINISTRATOR
Child Therapists	Mother/Toddler Coord.		Dir. of Dev./P. R.
Psychologists	Kindergarten Coord.		Admin. Assts.
Students	Day Care Consultant		Comm. Outreach Coor.
Group Home Staff			Clerical Staff
Social Workers			Transport. Superv.
Students			

respond much better to appeals from volunteers than from staff members.

Board members make policy decisions and appoint the executive director. They participate in a variety of committees, plan and execute changes in personnel policies, help with financial planning, and represent the agency during the legislative session. They serve as child advocates and keep the community abreast of the agency's doings. Due to the board, the agency's community relations have always been exceptionally good and contribute greatly to the Center's continuing expansion. Some of our most effective board members are former volunteers, intimately acquainted with the operation, the philosophy, and goals of the Center.

RESEARCH ADVISORY BOARD

The Children's Center Research Advisory Board consists of University of Utah faculty members in related fields. They serve as resource facilitators to the director of research and help in networking with the academic community.

ORGANIZATION OF THE AGENCY

Executive Director

The executive/medical director is in overall charge of the agency. She or he delegates administration and clinical services of the day-treatment centers to two clinical directors, who hire clinical day-care staff. One of them is also the chief psychologist; this individual, with the help of the psychology consultant, supervises the psychology trainees, interns, and residents. The other clinical director is the chief social worker, who supervises the social workers and, with the help of a consultant in social work, the social work students. The group home is under the direction of a social worker.

The staff providing auxiliary services is supervised by the medical director, as is the director of research. The medical director delegates some of this responsibility to the research advisory board.

Administrative Director

The administrative director is in charge of all budgeting, contractual agreements with state and local agencies, hiring and firing of nonclinical personnel, supervision of transportation staff, and maintenance of the buildings. This director works closely with the director of development and the community outreach coordinator.

Funding

Funding has been a major problem since the beginning of the agency. A concentrated effort was made not to rely on federal funding, because of its uncertainties, but to energize the community to finance day-treatment services for its young, emotionally disturbed children. The center has frequently operated on a shoestring budget, yet it has managed to maintain itself. In the early years a training grant from the W. C. Grant Foundation provided funds for trainees who served as child therapists, thus relieving the budget. In time the agency was admitted to the United Fund and obtained line-item contracts for service from the Department of Human Services. The guiding principle has always been first to identify a need in the community, to develop a program, and then to find the money for it. The total budget has been dependent on a great variety of funding sources.

The largest portion of the revenue needed comes through the local mental health authority, which is in charge of all Medicaid funds in the state of Utah. Other major funding is contributed by a variety of social service block grants. In addition, the United Way participates in the funding of several programs. The rest comes through contributions from foundations, corporations, and individuals; client fees; and investment income.

Director of Development and Public Relations

The director of development and public relations oversees all fundraising efforts, including the preparation of a variety of printed material explaining the agency's functions to the community, contributors, and professionals.

Community Outreach Coordinator

The community outreach coordinator recruits, trains, and oversees the volunteers. The ambassador for the agency in the community, the coordinator speaks to many groups and maintains the agency's image. The coordinator also purchases all materials and serves as a liaison between child therapists and volunteers.

Clerical Staff

The clerical staff is in charge of record keeping, appointment scheduling, and all the other manifold clerical jobs that are essential in the operation of such a large agency.

Bus Drivers

All the children are transported to the day-treatment centers, and a bevy of drivers are supervised and coordinated by a dispatcher. This is no mean endeavor during the winter in our mountainous territory.

In Summary

Administration of a large team is difficult and demands an organization where decisions are discussed before they are finalized. Every member needs to feel that he or she has input; members need to know that their ideas will be considered, recognizing, however, that the final decision rests with the executive director. The executive's role is often a lonely one, and wrong decisions are bound to be made, but this is the price paid by any agency operated in a democratic fashion. Being in the helping profession is a tremendous responsibility and needs the combined input and understanding of all members of the team.

Chapter 12
Volunteers

INTRODUCTION

Volunteers or aides in group of children with special needs are the extra pair of hands needed to make the programs work. Whether they come daily or once a week, they are a welcome relief for teachers and therapists, as well as a source of pleasure for the children. New ideas, fresh energy, and, at times, a more objective look at the children add to their usefulness.

All volunteers at The Children's Center work directly in the children's groups. They help to maintain the 1-to-2 ratio so essential for young children with behavioral problems. Their motives are manifold; some use the opportunity to gain credit for classes at the University of Utah or to discover whether they want to work with children as a career. Some high school students from alternative programs find participation in therapy groups more suited to their needs than a straight academic curriculum. Although they are frequently a challenge to the group therapists, on the whole they have worked out rather well.

College-trained women whose children are in junior high or high school and who want to maintain an interest in child development or psychology come to the Center with the aim of possibly returning to the workforce at a later time. In fact, many staff and board members initially joined the agency as volunteers. Volunteers form an important network for the many practical needs that an agency like The Children's Center has. Our monthly wish list reads like the inventory of a department store! Our volunteers are public relations ambassadors for early childhood education and mental health. They sit on allocation boards of planning, funding agencies and talk knowledgeably about the special emotional and physical needs of young children. In addition, they help neighbors and friends, who know of their work at The Children's Center, to find information.

All concerned gain from the relationships formed, and these are never one-sided. The volunteers take pride in the children's emotional, cognitive, and social achievements, soon realizing how important they are. In the volunteers the children find accepting adults who often serve as a trial balloon for forming relationships of less intensity than with a therapist: "If they like me, I can't be so bad." As expressed by our volunteer coordinator in a recent article, "People from different cultures, people from various age groups, people with similar and differing opinions [come], but all are people who care about children and who want to help" (Smith-Taylor, 1991). Male volunteers serve as particularly helpful role models for our little boys, who frequently live with a single mother and lack positive male interaction. They learn that macho television images are not all there is to being grown up.

TRAINING

All potential volunteers attend a two-hour orientation session that acquaints them with the agency in general and their role in particular. The history of The Children's Center, its advocacy role in the community, and its funding sources are reviewed. The organizational structure of the agency and its interdisciplinary character are outlined. Milieu therapy and the specific assignment of each discipline are discussed in connection with the daily program and admission procedures. The volunteers become acquainted with the various outreach activities like the mother-toddler Group, the kindergarten follow-up program, and daycare consultation. The Children's Center group home and the population it serves are described also. Time is spent on the theoretical framework of activity group therapy and its justification in the treatment of young, behaviorally disturbed children.

Reading lists and material prepared by the agency staff are distributed (see Appendix D). Most volunteers find the written material useful and refer to it during their time at the Center, at home, and at other volunteer placements. The concept of a therapeutic preschool is, for many, brand new and overwhelming.

The orientation session familiarizes volunteers with the characteristics of the children and families coming to the Center. Intervention strategies and their use are discussed and examples are given during this time. Normal emotional, intellectual, and social developmental steps are reviewed in identifying the children's most frequently occurring problem: lack of trust and attachment. The children's basic feelings of insecurity are often expressed in antisocial or withdrawn behavior patterns, and their ever-present fear of being overlooked, unloved, and abandoned necessitates consistent attendance. Children remember not only your presence but also your absences. These points are stressed in the orientation, and volunteers are asked to make an initial commitment of eight weeks.

Time is spent in the observation room, behind a one-way window, observing the children and the therapists' interventions with the volunteer coordinator, who elaborates and explains the reasons for them.

Two areas of behavior are most difficult for volunteers to handle: the use of four-letter words in astonishing combinations, and the many seemingly unprovoked instances of aggression. Young children's vocabulary of four-letter words is astounding and upsetting to many volunteers. Children repeat the language they hear at home or in the neighborhood, often unaware of its significance or meaning. By preparing volunteers for the children's inappropriate language, we hope to avoid any shock effect. The adult's reaction may be firm, such as "We don't use these words here" or a turning away, but it must not be punitive and personal. Children used to gaining negative attention will quickly recognize the impact of their words and repeat the behavior to the consternation of the volunteer. The children's exaggerated use of physical aggression as conflict resolution is difficult to accept. They learn much of it through television, even just watching the news. Ours is a violent society, yet we do not like to see children model the violence they see, and the natural tendency is to say, "This is not nice. Say you are sorry." Most children are not sorry but angry, and they need to learn that being angry is okay, but hitting or biting is not. The therapists' interventions stress that other ways have to be used to show one's feelings. This is not an easy concept to learn, and many a volunteer disagrees with our handling. However, the aim of therapy is not the creation of guilt but the creation of appropriate adaptation to situations occurring with peers and adults.

During the course of the year, the volunteer coordinator meets with the volunteers to answer questions and discuss the input of various professionals at the Center. Several times a year half-day workshops are conducted by various staff members.

Once the volunteers are in the rooms with the children, it is up to the therapists to help them understand the Center's intervention strategies. Many of them can and are used at jobs or in their home. Volunteers are staff members and as such are encouraged to ask questions about the program and about specific interactions with the children. Volunteers sometimes want to know more about the children's backgrounds, their families, and other circumstances. This we cannot do, as it is very important to maintain confidentiality; however, the children's individual treatment goals are discussed to help volunteers understand interventions used. Although a good deal of progress has been made in the acceptance of emotional problems, the stigma still surrounds young children. It is invariably looked upon as a reflection on the parents, usually the mother's failure. Many parents are guilt-ridden at the thought of being unable to manage their young children and needing intervention, but they do not wish their neighbors to know about it. Incidents children bring up relating to home situations need to be forgotten.

Some volunteers are too shy to voice their surprise or even their misgivings at the children's behavior and need to be encouraged to express their feelings. Expression of feelings is healthy not just for the children but also for the adults working with them

Through getting acquainted with staff, volunteers form friendships and discover their special talents that add to the program and the volunteers' positive feelings about their contribution.

The myths of the "enchanted years" of childhood are sometimes difficult to discard, particularly if the children look as innocent as many of the ones attending The Children's Center.

GENERAL SUGGESTIONS GIVEN TO VOLUNTEERS

Speak in a calm, low voice. Use short, meaningful sentences the child can understand.

Try to express your request in a positive way. This will help the child to learn a better or more acceptable way of responding.

Have fun! Bring your sense of humor with you.

Try to put yourself on a physical level with the children. Sit on the floor when they are engaged in play there, or on a chair when they are at a table or water table. Wear comfortable, easily cleaned clothing. You are more apt to join in if you're not worried about soiling your clothes.

Cleanup can be a difficult time. You can encourage the children by saying, "Show me what you're going to put away next," by helping with the cleanup yourself, or by getting a "moving van" (truck). Help clean up between activities. This is a shared responsibility among the adults in the group. Mostly it will mean wiping off the table to prepare it for the next activity.

Generally, it is not a good idea to talk with children about their families unless they initiate the conversation, since a number of our children do not live with their natural parents. If you are in over your head, ask a therapist for assistance or support, including the child in the process. The child will then see that you and the therapists are a team. Please feel free to ask questions if you have any doubt about how to handle a situation.

The therapist or co-therapist will handle all extremely disruptive behavior: throwing things, hitting, biting, scratching, tantrums. You can intervene to protect a child, saying, "We don't hit (throw) things." If a child hits you, be honest and say that you don't like to be hit, it hurts, and so on. Your facial expression should match what you are saying. Ignore all tantrums, swearing, and stuttering. When something negative is happening, it is often good to comment on some positive activity going on in the room.

Do not pay special attention to an individual child by bringing presents or making something for a child to take home. Such special treatment will isolate you and the child from the rest of the children.

Do not compare one child with another child by saying, "See how clean Jim's hands are." This might make the child dislike both Jim and you.

During book and puzzle time, adults in the room read books to children individually and in small groups. They also help them with the puzzles they are doing. This is a good time to be involved with individual children and to encourage physical contact, for example, allowing a child to sit on an adult's lap or next to him or her.

Lunch time should be calm and free of stress and tension. You can encourage slow eaters by saying, "Show me what you're going to eat next." Bring your lunch to provide a model. Children who talk with their mouths full can be told, "I'd like to talk to you as soon as you swallow your food." Spills should be handled right away by the children. The children can get a sponge or towel from the sink and clean up the spill with minimal adult assistance.

During outside play time, it is very important to have an adult near each play area—sandbox, slide, climbing gym, and so on. Keep involved and enjoy yourself! Organize games to help children remain constructively engaged and to provide success experiences. Avoid spending time with the other adults.

Art is a time for the therapists to see the children's progress in specific skills such as following instructions, cutting, or holding a pencil. During art activities, give the least amount of help necessary to each child. Art should be left for the child to create, not the adult. Avoid making models in any art medium for the children to copy. If a child asks you to draw something, suggest that you draw together, following the child's lead. If children ask you to write their name, you can dot the name on the reverse side of the art project (first letter capital, rest small letters) for them to copy.

Rug (circle) time demands attention that is difficult for many children to maintain. Keep the child's attention focused on the person who is talking, reading, or singing. Do not let the child engage you in conversation. It is helpful to point to the person talking and say, "It's time to listen to ———— now." Encourage the child to sit by himself or herself rather than to lean on you. The best way to handle this situation is to move away from the child and ignore it. Participate in the activities, the songs, the fingerplays, and the like, even if you don't know the words.

Inside free play might look confusing to you. Ask the therapists why it is done. You can help to keep the noise level down by encouraging the children to "use your inside voice" or by saying, "I can hear you better when it's quiet."

Sharing toys, defending toys, and saving toys represent a significant, but often difficult, part of free play. Encourage the children to resolve these matters by themselves. If a child wants a turn with a toy that another child has, prompt the youngster to say, "Can I have a turn?" or "I want a turn in five minutes." You can watch the time and indicate when time is up.

If another child is trying to take toys away, prompt a child to defend the toys with, "You can tell Betty to stop" or "I don't like that." Intervene physically only if children become aggressive toward each other. You should facilitate, not solve the problem for the child. Generally, save toys for children only if they need to use the bathroom.

In private, nonprofit agencies, the role of volunteers cannot be overestimated. For they provide all the additional input that budgets do not permit.

Appendix A

Assessment Considerations—Developmental Vulnerabilities
by Barbara Kalmanson

Stages of Development	Self Organization	Social-Emotional	Motor	Sensory Integration	Language
Infancy	-Difficulty with regulation of states, Irritability, crying, trouble falling asleep -Attention seems random, not focused or responsive to adult interaction	-Unresponsive -Lack of reciprocal gaze -Absence of anticipatory response to being held -Seems to prefer to be alone -Fails to form strong personal attachments	-Lack of motor response to voice -Arches back when held -Doesn't mold to parent's body, limp	-Easily upset by extraneous sounds/sights, startles, easily -Trouble coordinating input from parents (Can't look at mother while being held & talked to)	-Absence of cooing in response to parents' vocalizations -Lack of attention to parents voice
Toddler-hood	-Little organized attention to people or objects -Difficulty falling asleep wakes up irritable -Irregular food intake	-Little or no reciprocal interaction/play -Little attachment to primary caregivers -Indifference or extreme prolonged distress at comings or goings of primary caregivers -Absence of imitative play	-Disorganized, random movement -Impulsive racing and falling -Apathetic - little interest in movement	-Easily startled -Doesn't localize sound -Overwhelmed by moderate stimulation and withdraws -Engages in self-stimulation	-Absence of communication/gestures -Little imitation of words -No words for important people/objects -Lack of intentionality in communication

Preschool	-Attention span of less than 5 min. for self-selected tasks -Highly distractible -Trouble modulating stimulation; easily overwhelmed; "falls apart" "tantrums" -Irregular behavior patterns - sleeping, eating, toileting	-Little interest in peers &/or adults -Prefers solitary play -Little self-control -Extreme dependance on adult assistance -Ritualistic -Absence of representational play	-Extremely active; falls frequently; doesn't know where body is going -Apathetic - stays in one place for long periods (doesn't climb, can't turn doorknob)	-Trouble alternating attention to person & object -Trouble joining group activities -Absence of representational drawing -Poor tool use -Stilted, repetitive use of words -Absence of spontaneous language	-Inability to clearly make needs/wants known -Absence of conversational language
K-entry	-Trouble attending to tasks for more than a few moments -Trouble taking direction from an adult -Difficulty with transitions -Dependence on adult assistance for dressing eating, toileting, falling asleep -Irregular patterns of behavior -Moodiness	-Relationships with peers &/or adults peripheral or lack depth -No recognition of rules, standards for right & wrong -Overwhelmed or paralyzed by fears -Poor modulation of aggression -Cries easily & inconsolably -Extreme social inhibition or bravado	-Reckless or fearful about large motor tasks -Poor coordination; no skipping, hopping -Little attention to appropriate motor control	-Poor eye-hand coordination -Difficulty following patterns for visual or auditory sequences (clapping/block designs) -Doesn't draw a recognizable person -Can't follow teacher's directions	-Little or no language for self expression of feelings -Inability to carry on a conversation or tell a story

Age-Level Behavior Chart

THE TWO-YEAR-OLD

Self-Care:

Toilet training begun
Puts on/takes off shoes, socks, coat, hat
Unbuttons
Unzips zipper
Washes/dries hands with some help
Eats with a spoon

Speech:

Fifty-word vocabulary of common objects
Knows four body parts, e.g., eyes, ears, nose, mouth, hair, feet
Follows commands
Uses two- to four-word phrases
Refers to self by name
Uses wide variety of sounds
Associates their use with objects (Which one do you eat with?)

Small Motor:

Builds tower of six cubes
Can roll, pound, squeeze, pull clay
Fills/dumps containers with sand

Large Motor:

Walks/runs well
Jumps in place
Mounts trike with assistance
Walks approximately on a line

Ascends/descends stairs (nonalternating)
Walks on tiptoes

Cognitive:

Joins in nursery rhymes/songs
Locates two objects hidden while child watches
Responds to two out of three commands
Matches shapes—circle, square, triangle
Repeats two digits

Social-Emotional:

Developed sense of trust—can leave mother
Has short play span with other children
Afraid of loud noises
Occasional temper tantrums
Independent—"Me do it!"
Asserts his or her own will

Play Reactions:

Engages in tug-of-war over materials
Is possessive of things but not jealous
Likes humorous games such as Peek-a-Boo, chasing, and others
Starts and continues games without adult suggestion

Fears:

Mother leaving, especially at bedtime
Rain
Wind
Animals
Loud noises—trucks, trains
Large buildings
Large objects
Changes such as moving to a new home to live or changed room

Personal Characteristics:

Peak age of disequilibrium, rigid, inflexible, demanding, attached to old things,
   routine, mood swings

THE THREE-YEAR-OLD

Self-Care:

Buttons one to two buttons
Feeds self with little spilling

Small Motor:

Strings four or more beads
Paints strokes, dots, circular shapes on easel
Copies a circle

Cognitive:

Follows two-part directions
Matches colors—red, blue, green, yellow
Identifies action in pictures
Identifies fingers, toes, stomach, knee, back
Knows full name

Speech:

Uses the following sounds correctly: *P, M, H, N, W, B*
Follows two-part directions (i.e., give me the block; close the door)
Uses plurals
Knows a few rhymes
Vocabulary of about 1,000 words

Large Motor:

Pedals trike
Stands on one foot holding a support
Hops on one foot two or more times
Walks forward five steps on balance beam
Ascends stairs with alternating feet

Social-Emotional:

Attempts more cooperative play
Adjusts to taking turns
Likes to please
Imitative
Uses *I*
Likes sounds, nonsense words
Attention span of ten to fifteen minutes

Play Reactions:

Can play twenty to thirty minutes
Still inclined to strike out at person or obstacle
Shifts identity to animals
"Beats" or bosses imaginary playmates, which helps his learning in emotional
   adjustment

Fears:

Mostly visual—masks, the dark, animals, worries about Mother and Daddy
   going out at night

General Reactions:

Likes praise, likes to please
Responds to whispering
Imaginative, alert
Interested in persons
Likes to conform, share, give and take
Interested in language use

Signs of Trouble:

Persistent wetting/soiling
Persistent eating problems
Nonspeaking
Body rocking
Finger sucking
Withdrawal, isolation from peers
Inability to follow two directions
Refusal of affection
Persistent sadness
Excessive crying

THE THREE-AND-A-HALF-YEAR-OLD

Becomes poorly coordinated
Often stutters
Has difficulty relating to people
Demanding

NEEDS FOR OPTIMAL EMOTIONAL DEVELOPMENT:

Adults who consistently accept expression of anger, and offer pretend play and
alternative expression if indicated

THE FOUR-YEAR-OLD

Self-Care:

Puts on shoes
Undresses/dresses self
Closes front snaps
Usually stays dry all night

Speech:

Uses the following sounds correctly: K, G, D, T, F, Y
Uses mostly complete sentences
Can relate an experience
Asks many questions
1,500-word vocabulary

Large Motor:

Ascends/descends stairs using alternating feet
Beginning to learn to skip

Small Motor:

Cuts with blunt scissors
Drives nails and pegs
Puts together a seven-piece puzzle
Copies a cross
Copies oblique lines
Draws people with a head and two appendages

Cognitive:

Obeys three to five prepositions: on top of, under, inside, over, out
Participates in storytelling
Tells age and sex
Names own drawing
Matches pictures
Counts to three
Differentiates between *one* and *many*
Can find pictures of animals that are alike
Names objects from memory (hide one of three objects)
Understands some opposites—boy/girl, day/night, up/down
Can identify pictures that are the same or different
Follows a series of three directions

Social-Emotional:

Is imaginative, shows initiative
Is creative, has interests outside of home
Plays cooperatively
Can be easily frustrated
Expects much from himself or herself

Personal Characteristics:

Assertive
Dogmatic
Boastful
Bossy
Independent
Cooperative
Inquisitive
Imitative
Explosive (becomes so easily)
Tearful
Quarrelsome
Argumentative
Impatient

Selfish
Silly

Play Reactions:

Needs children as playmates
Is more interested in children than in adults
Will share or play cooperatively with special friends
Shows better socialization in groups
Practices much excluding, tattling, disputing, quarreling—both verbal and
    physical (emotional reaction)
Can play well imaginatively
Talkative
Needs guidance and plenty of materials, otherwise whines
Is physically aggressive—bites, kicks, throws, hits
Is verbally aggressive
Plays with toys roughly and carelessly
Laughs wildly during play

General Reactions:

Is full of alibis
Prefers being with own sex
Shows very little politeness unless prompted
Shows off and acts very badly before company
Likes to be mother or teacher to a shy child
Finds it hard to share
Won't take forcing
Is frustrated by not being able to do what he or she wishes—tantrums
Is jealous of siblings or of Mom and Dad together
Uses "toilet" talk
Likes imaginary companions, tall tales

Signs of Trouble:

Isolation
Lack of speech
Unwillingness to try new skills
Toileting problems
Running away
Accident proneness
Unwillingness to leave parent

THE FIVE-YEAR-OLD

Self-Care:

Attempts to cut food
Buttons four buttons
Begins to lace shoes

Speech:

Follows three successive commands
2,000-word vocabulary
Indicates past and future tenses correctly in some instances
Uses objective pronouns (him, her) correctly

Small Motor:

Draws simple house
Prints capital initials of own name
Uses crayon easily
Draws recognizable man
Copies a square
Is beginning to copy a triangle

Large Motor:

Beginning to be able to move both arms and legs together (jumping jacks or
    angels in the snow)
Beginning to alternate feet in skipping
Balances on one foot for ten seconds

Cognitive:

Obeys four prepositions
"Reads" pictures
Can discuss pictorial likenesses and differences
Groups objects: food, animals, toys
Can make opposite analogies
Beginning to distinguish between left and right
Names colors correctly

Social-Emotional:

Proud of being five
Very social
Initiative in play
Likes friends and shares
Persistence in learning new skills
Eager for new experiences
Abundance of energy
Good sense of humor

Personal Characteristics:

Is proud
Self-sufficient
Social
Friendly
Self-contained
Humorous
Helpful
Endearing

Sympathetic
Reliable
Less demanding
Likes to learn new things

Play Reactions:

Is usually able to manage in social groups without conflict
Plays best cooperatively with only three
Feels protective toward younger ones in group
Does not insist on his or her own way
Is less bossy than at four
Plans surprises and jokes
Is better in outdoor play than indoor
Prefers playmates of the same age
Plays well and happily—few conflicts

Signs of Trouble:

No friends
Won't share
Lack of curiosity
Controlling
Oppositional
Won't go to bed

THE SIX-YEAR-OLD

Emotional—functions at opposite extremes, loves one minute, hates the next
Whatever is wrong, others are blamed
Demanding of others and rigid in those demands—cannot adapt
Vigorous and energetic and ready for anything new
Wants all of everything
Difficult to choose between two alternatives
Most difficult for him or her to accept criticism, blame, punishment
Peer group becoming important

THE SEVEN-YEAR-OLD

More withdrawn age
More likely to complain than rejoice
Morose, mopey, and moody
Likes to be alone
Likes to watch, listen, stay on the edge of any scene
Hands keep busy touching, exploring, feeling everything
Intellect is in the ascendancy
Often demands too much of self—aware of the task but not able to complete it
Needs help in defining limits
Has good days and bad days—learning days and forgetting everything days
Tends to feel everyone is against him or her—"nobody loves me" attitude

Appendix C
Excerpts from: "Some Observations Regarding Group Psychotherapy with Young Children"

While serving as an intern at The Children's Center this fall, I have been struggling to conceptualize the small group of eight disturbed preschool children I am working with as a psychotherapy group. In many ways, this group resembles a regular nursery school group. The group activities consist mostly of work with puzzles, looking at books, cutting out shapes, social, and imaginative play (including indoor and outdoor free play with materials like sand, snow, water, or salt in a tub), art, music, eating lunch, and an occasional field trip. However, I have observed some differences between the therapy group at The Children's Center and a regular nursery school group. I will first attempt to sort out which of the differences might be explained by the fact that one group is a therapy group and then will arrive at a definition of group psychotherapy with young children.

At The Children's Center, children are carefully placed together in groups so that their behavioral patterns or strengths and weaknesses are somewhat complementary and will result, over time, in moving toward a common ground through modeling effects and other kinds of social learning. Behavioral standards and expectations for groups at The Children's Center are clear, crystallized, and explicit. Behavioral standards are consistently supported through the use of reinforcement by the adults. After the children have been in the group for two or three sessions, they begin to model the adults—for example, by ignoring a child who is having a tantrum or moving away from aggressors. Positive reinforcement of desired behavior is used more frequently by the adults than ignoring of undesirable behaviors. Some of the standards are: 1) dress yourself without help except for shoelaces and sometimes boots, 2) sit in your chair while eating, 3) use a person's name when you want to get their attention, 4) don't hit people, 5) listen when people talk to you, 6) look at people when they are talking to you or you are talking to them, 7) try new things, and 8) play with the other children.

New children in the group look surprised and puzzled by some of these behavioral expectations. One day a child had a temper tantrum and no one paid any attention to him. Two children who had only been in the group one week looked at the child, and then at all the other people in the group. Both children asked, "Why is he over there all alone?" The therapist answered, "Sometimes it helps kids who are having a problem if we leave them alone." Another day, one of the new children began hitting two of the adults and knocked over a chair. He was separated from the others by about four feet for a couple of minutes and told, "You can use words. I don't like to be hit." He then bent over and spanked himself! Apparently, this child had every expectation of a spanking, and when he didn't receive one, he just filled in the missing blank. At that moment, he began to understand that things in the group are different from home.

For most children, standards and expectations for behavior at The Children's Center are indeed different from expectations at home. They are also very consistently reinforced, and adult behaviors are always consistent with them. For example, consistent with the standard about not hitting others, an adult would not spank a child. Children learn the behavioral standards and adult expectations through modeling, explicit statements, reinforcement, and sanctions. Behaving in accordance with them is an essential, central part of therapeutic change for the child. The parents participate through regular appointments with counseling staff and are encouraged to observe their child in group.

In The Children's Center group, the therapists play a directive, parent-type role. They respect each child and his or her behavior, and the standards they establish and reinforce reflect their belief that children are capable of change and growth, and specifically of doing the things expected of them. By their consistency and explicitness, the therapists foster the development of mutual trust. By their liberal use of verbal and nonverbal social reinforcers and, on occasion primary reinforcers, they create warm relationships with the children. Transference is evident very early in the sense that the children expect the therapists to act like their parents. In fact, both of the new children mentioned above were calling one female therapist and one volunteer "Mom" by their third session. The group is very helpful both in catalyzing the new child's approach to the therapist (the newness and frequency of social interaction with peers probably make new children anxious and intensify their need to form a relationship with the leader/therapist) and providing models for how to do this.

As the group at The Children's Center has developed throughout the fall, it has progressed through the following states: 1) initial testing, 2) leader dependence, 3) plateau, 4) peer relationship development, 5) fantasy and play, and 6) self direction. The group as a whole is currently in about stage 6. However, this is an open-ended group and the newer children are still in the first three stages. Each child seems to progress through these stages at an individual rate. The more disorganized child spends more time in initial testing, for example. The stages are not discrete for any child or for the group as a whole. There is plenty of backsliding and jumping ahead, but it is easy to see a kind of basic settling in one predominant stage.

The same factors discussed above operate in most normal nursery school groups, and in groups in general. What distinguishes the therapy group at The

Table C.1

Differences Observed between Groups in a Therapeutic Program and a Regular Nursery School

The Children's Center	Regular Nursery School
Close attention to composition of group; children are placed together to achieve therapeutic balance.	Moderate attention to composition of group; children are placed together according to general developmental progress so group curriculum and activities will be appropriate for all.
Behavioral standards cover a wide range of behaviors and are explicit and clear.	Behavioral standards are not explicit and children seem unaware of rules to guide their behavior. Teachers intervene to stop unacceptable behavior only when it becomes disruptive to the whole group. Intervention usually consists of redirecting child to other activity without being explicit about what child did wrong or what constitutes right behavior.
Maximum group size is 9; ratio of adults to children is 1:2.	Maximum group size is 16; ratio of adults to children is about 1:5.
Leaders are directive. While children have many opportunities to choose, leaders intervene if choice is inappropriate for child in terms of individual therapeutic goals.	Leaders do not appear knowledgeable about specific behavior management techniques. Not one instance was observed of positive reinforcement for a specific desired behavior such as cooperative play.
Psychological and behavioral assessment precede placement.	Psychological and behavioral assessment do not precede placement.

Table C.1 (continued)

Individual therapeutic goals are set for each child and reviewed every two weeks, providing continuous assessment of progress. Goals are specific and measurable, and always represent small steps on way to larger goals.	Individual goals are set for each child periodically in very general terms such as "encourage cooperative play." Assessment of progress is attempted in a general way: "Not there yet; continue to encourage cooperative play."
Primary concern is with helping each child make rapid progress on individual therapeutic goals. When this fails to occur, leaders and supervisor brainstorm possible interventions.	Primary concern is with developmental curriculum.
Reinforcement is generally contingent upon adherence to behavioral norms or standards. Social reinforcers are used very frequently for positive behaviors.	Social reinforcers (e.g., paying attention, touching, praise) are used frequently, but indiscriminately, and without design. Sometimes "bad" behaviors are inadvertently reinforced.
Therapeutic focus.	Educational focus.

Children's Center from a regular nursery school group? To answer this, I observed a single nursery school group several times for comparison. Some of the observed differences are described in Table C.1.

Not all of the differences described between the groups of children at The Children's Center and a regular nursery school are due simply to the fact that one is a therapeutic group and the other is not. Some programs for young children, such as the regular nursery school observed, believe in permissiveness and the power of unconditional positive regard. Each child is expected to unfold or fulfill his or her potential in a healthy way under these conditions. A wide range of materials and activities, ranging from simple to complex, is available for the child to choose from with little direction. The teachers may feel that if a child is aggressive, this is due to tension and anxiety, and attempts to prohibit aggression might have the effect of capping a volcano, with the result that the child's tension and anxiety will seek expression in other ways. Aggression is thus to be handled through unconditional positive regard and a permissive atmosphere. At The Children's Center, efforts are begun from the first day to help a child with poor impulse control by setting safe limits. Children are encouraged to release tension by talking directly about their anger when they are mad at someone—, "Stop it. I don't like that. It hurts my ears." Interpretations are given to children who are behaving in ways which reveal anger, sadness, etc., so that they may recognize their feelings and then deal with them in a more appropriate manner. Unacceptable aggressive behavior leads to immediate consequences, and alternative, acceptable behaviors are taught and modeled on the spot. Thus, some of the differences described in Table A.1 are the result of differing theoretical orientations regarding the psychological development of young children and their behavioral repertories.

The dimensions which seem to define and be unique to the therapy group are: 1) The primary focus in the therapy group is on the needs of the individual children. The group is arranged so that each member's needs can be served appropriately. As a result, group composition and group needs are fairly consistent with individual needs. 2) Careful psychological and behavioral assessment of each individual child prior to placement serves as the basis for the development of therapeutic goals. 3) Group activities and therapist behaviors are planned to meet the therapeutic goals both of each child in the group and of the group as a whole. 4) The progress of each child is continuously monitored, and goals are reviewed and refined formally every two weeks. Lack of progress is cause for immediate concern, and appropriate interventions are discussed and developed. 5) The therapist does not allow self-interest and personal needs to operate at a level customary in ordinary social interaction. Rather, the therapists subordinate their own needs and modify their own behavior to meet the needs of the children.

Group psychotherapy with young children is a formal process calculated to bring about desired behavioral changes and social/emotional growth.

Nicki N. Ostrom

Appendix D
Reading List

Adams, P. (1974). *A primer of child psychotherapy.* New York: Little, Brown.

Allen, F. (1942). *Psychotherapy with children.* New York: W. W. Norton.

Axline, V. (1969). *Play therapy.* New York: Ballantine.

Briggs, D. C. (1970). *Your child's self-esteem: The key to his life.* New York: Doubleday.

Coles, R. (1967). *Children of crisis.* Boston: Little, Brown.

Cooper, S., and Wanerman, L. (1977). *Children in treatment.* New York: Bruner/Mazel.

Erickson, E. (1950). *Childhood and society.* New York: W. W. Norton.

Fraiberg, S. (1959). *The magic years.* New York: Scribner.

Karen, R. (1990, February). Becoming attached. *The Atlantic Monthly.*

Landy, S., and Peters, R. D. (1991). Understanding and treating the hyperaggressive toddler. *Zero to Three, 11*(3).

Marzollo, J., and Lloyd, J. (1972). *Learning through play.* New York: Harper & Row.

Plenk, A. M. (1982). *PST—Plenk Storytelling Test.* Salt Lake City, UT: The Children's Center.

Plenk, A. M. (1978, May). Activity group therapy for emotionally disturbed preschool children. *Behavior Disorders, 3*(3).

Plenk, A. M., and Hinchey, F. S. (1985, March-April). Clinical assessment of maladjusted preschool children. *Child Welfare, 64*(2).

Redl, F. (1966). *When we deal with children.* Glencoe, IL: Free Press.

Satir, V. (1972). *People making.* Palo Alto, CA: Science & Behavior Books.

Schaefer, C. E. (Ed.). (1976). *Therapeutic use of child's play.* New York: Jason Aronson.

Schorr, L. B., and Schorr, D. (1988–89). *Within our reach.* New York: Doubleday.

Thomas, A., and Chess, S. (1986). *Temperament in clinical practice.* New York: Guilford Press.

Whittaker, J. K. (1974). Program activities: Their selection and use in a thera-
     peutic milieu. In P. Glasser, R. Sarri, and R. Vitner (Eds.), *Individual
     change through small groups.* New York: Free Press.
Wood, M. (Ed.). (1975). *Developmental therapy.* Baltimore, MD: University
     Park Press.

Appendix E
Program Activities

OUTDOOR

Ages 3 - 5

ACTIVITY	PRESCRIPTIVENESS	CONTROL	MOVEMENT	REWARDS	COMPETENCE	INTERACTION
Trikes	m	l	h	h	h/m	l
Slide	h	l	h	h	m	m/l
Swing	h	l	h	h	h	l
Stepping	l	l	h	h/m	h/m	l
Tricky Bars	h	l	h	h	h	l
Teeter-totter	h	h	h	h	h	h
Sand/Snow	l	l	l	h	l	l
Ball-kicking	m	l	h	h	h	l
-catch	m	m	h	h	h	m
-basketball	h	h	h	h	h	l
Ice Skating	h	l	h	h	h	l
Chase	l	l	m	h	l	h
Pool Activities	h	l	h	h	h	l
Hiking	l	l	m	m/l	l	m
Snow Sledding	h	l	m	h	m	l
Collecting	l	l	m	h	l	l
Plant Gardens	h	h	m	l	h/m	l
Running	l	l	h	l	m	l
Exercises	l	h	h	l	h	l

188

INDOOR

Ages 3 - 5

ACTIVITY	PRESCRIPTIVENESS	CONTROL	MOVEMENT	REWARDS	COMPETENCE	INTERACTION
Bean Bags	m	l	m	h	l	l
Water Table	l	l	l	h	l	l
Blocks	m	l	l	h	m	l
Puzzles	h	h	l	h	h	l
Paints	m	l	l	h	m	l
Finger-paint	m	l	l	h	l	l
Cutting	m	l	h	h	h	l
Pasting	l	m	l	h	m	l
Stringing	m	h	h	h	h	l
Play Dough	l	l	l	h	l	l
Cooking	h	h	l	h	m	l
Cognitive Grouping	h	h	l	h	h	l
Coloring	l	l	h	h	h	l
Trucks/Cars	h	l	m	h	l	l
Dolls	l	l	l	h	l	l
Dress-up	l	l	l	h	l	l

GROUP
Ages 3 – 5

ACTIVITY	PRESCRIPTIVENESS	CONTROL	MOVEMENT	REWARDS	COMPETENCE	INTERACTION
Stories	l	h	l	m	h	l
Singing	l	m	m	h	m	h
Rhythm Instruments	m	m	m	h	m	h
Marching	l	h	h	m	h/m	h
Memory Games	l	h	l	h	h	l
Singing Games	l	h	h	h	l	h

l = low

m = medium

h = high

Appendix F
Evaluation Form

To facilitate report writing, the following outline is suggested.

Physical Appearance
Use of body
Facial expressions

Speech
Language use
Quality of voice
Vocabulary
Volume

Types of Play
Solitary
Watching
Parallel
Interactive
Cooperative
Disruptive
Symbolic

Approach to materials
Hesitant
Distant
Fearful

Immediate
Direct
With curiosity

Choice of Materials
Diversified
Stereotyped
Original
Imitative

Use of Materials
Appropriately
Idiosyncratically
For social outreach
For isolation

EMOTIONAL INTERACTIONS

Between child and child (positive, negative, hostile, none)
Between child and adult (appropriate, casual, demanding, friendly,
   indifferent, scared, avoidant)
Coping with crisis
General affect

Self-Care
Eating
Toileting
Dressing
Washing/Drying hands
Nailbiting
Rocking
Masturbation
Thumbsucking

Small Motor
Hold scissors
Cut (straight line, circle, etc.)
Paste
Scribble
Color
Creative
Laterality

Large Motor
Runs
Climbs
Throws ball
Pedals trike

Speech
Vocabulary
Listening baby talk
Mute
Sounds substitutions
Volume
Can recognize sounds

Affect
Appropriate
Overstimulated
Inappropriate
Range
Intensity

Group Activities
Joins readily
Reluctantly
Refuses
Tantrums
Favorite activity

Interactions with Adults
Warm, responsive
Distant, fearful
Pushy
Hard time with limits
Dependent
Manipulative

Interaction with Children
Stays away
Grabby or pushy
Can't defend himself
Reaches out positively
Reaches out negatively
Can't share

Coping with Crisis
Falls apart
Asks for help
Withdraws
Handles crisis himself

Intellectual Performance
Attention span—
  skills
Perseveration
Comprehension
Colors and shapes

General Behavior
Gets easily
Tunes out
Hyperactive
Withdrawn
Retires with one toy

Free Play
Lost and quiet
Overactive
Persevering
Creative
Isolated
Favorite toy

Impulse Control
Indoors
Outdoors

Strengths
Intellectual
Social

Appendix G
Suggestions to Volunteers

It's Better to Say	Than
Sit down when you slide.	Don't stand up when you slide.
Let's dig in the sand.	Don't throw the sand.
Let's sit in the swing.	Don't stand in the swing.
Use both hands when you climb.	You'll fall if you don't watch out.
Climb down the ladder.	Don't jump off the box.
Let's keep the puzzle on the table.	Don't dump the puzzle pieces on the floor.
Please use your inside voice.	Don't shout.
Turn the page carefully.	Don't tear the book.
Wipe your hands on the paper towel.	Don't put your hand on anything.
Let me hold the ladder.	Be careful, you might fall.
We sit on chairs.	Don't rock on your chair.
Move back on your rug, there...	Don't lean forward so that the other children can't see.
Wipe your brush on the jar.	Don't drip paint on the floor.
We all put aprons on.	Don't you want to put an apron on?
Time to go inside now.	Shall we go inside?
Wash your hands.	Don't you want to wash your hands?
Drink your milk.	Don't you want your milk?

Bibliography

Abidin, R. R. (1986). *Parental Stress Index* (2nd ed.). Charlottsville, VA: Pediatric Psychology Press.

Achenbach, T. M., & Edelbrock, C. (1983). *Manual for the Child Behavior Checklist and Revised Child Behavior Profile.* Burlington: University of Vermont, Department of Psychiatry.

Adams, P. (1974). *A Primer of Child Psychiatry.* New York: Little, Brown.

Ainsworth, M. D. (1982). Early caregiving and later patterns of attachment. *Birth, Interaction and Attachment.* Johnson and Johnson Baby Products.

Ainsworth, M. D., Blehon, M., Walter, T., & Walls, S. (1979). *Patterns of Attachment,* Hillsdale, NJ: Lawrence Erlbaum.

Allen, F. (1942). *Psychotherapy with Children.* New York: W. W. Norton.

Aronson, E. (1966, September 11). Try a little dissonance. *New York Times.*

Ashton-Warner, S. (1963). *Teacher.* New York: Simon & Schuster.

Axline, V. (1964). Accepting the child completely. In M. R. Haworth (Ed.), *Child Psychotherapy* (239–242). New York: Basic Books.

Axline, V. (1964). Recognition and reflection of feeling. In M. R. Haworth (Ed.), *Child Psychotherapy* (262–264). New York: Basic Books.

Axline, V. (1969). *Play Therapy.* New York: Ballantine.

Bailey, N. (1969). *Manual for the Bailey Scale of Infant Development.* New York: Psychological Corp.

Beery, K. E. (1982). *Developmental Test of Visual Motor Integration–Revised.* Chicago: Follett Educational Corp.

Bellak, L., & Adelman, C. (1960). The Children's Apperception Test. In A. I. Rabin and M. R. Haworth, *Projective Techniques with Children* (62–95). New York: Grune & Stratton.

Bender, L. (1946). *The Bender Gestalt Test.* San Antonio, TX: Psychological Corp.

Berman, C., & Lourie, I. S. (1988). Mental health issues in early intervention programs. *OSERS, 1*(4)(9).

Bettelheim, B. (1987). The importance of play. *Atlantic Monthly,* 35–43. Boulder, CO.

Biber, B. (1984). *Education and Psychological Development.* New Haven, CT: Yale University Press.

Bolster, E. R., & Wood, M. M. (1975). Management strategies and verbal techniques which bring therapeutic results. In M. M. Wood (Ed.), *Developmental Therapy* (105–127). Baltimore: University Park Press.

Bowlby, J. (1988). *A Secure Base: Parent-Child Attachment and Healthy Human Development.* New York: Basic Books.

Briggs, D. C. (1970). *Your Child's Self-Esteem: The Key to His Life.* New York: Doubleday & Company.

Bruch, H. (1948). The role of the parent in psychotherapy with children. *Psychiatry, 11:*169–175.

Bruch, H. (1974). *Learning Psychotherapy.* Cambridge, Mass: Harvard University Press.

Buckley, H. E. (1961, October). The little boy (poem). *School Arts Magazine.*

Burns, R. C., & Kaufman, S. H. (1972). *Actions, Styles and Symbols in Kinetic Family Drawing.* New York: Bruner/Mazel.

Carbonara, N. (1961). Techniques for observing normal child behavior. Pittsburgh: Arsenal Family and Children's Center, University of Pittsburgh.

Cohen, D., & Stern, V. (1958). *Observing and Recording the Behavior of Young Children.* New York Teacher's College: Columbia University.

Coles, R. (1967). *Children of Crisis.* Boston: Little, Brown.

Coles, R. (1992). *Anna Freud: The Dream of Psychoanalysis.* Reading, Mass: Addison-Wesley.

Cooper, S., & Wanerman, L. (1977). *Children in Treatment: A Primer for Beginning Psychotherapists.* New York: Brunner/Mazel.

DiLeo, J. H. (1973). *Children's Drawings as Diagnostic Aids.* New York: Brunner/Mazel.

Dinnage, R. (1988). *One to One Experiences of Psychotherapy.* New York: Viking.

Dulcan, M. K. (1984). Brief psychotherapy with children and their families: The state of the art. *Journal of the American Academy of Child Psychiatry, 23*(5): 544–551.

Dunn, L. M., & Dunn, L. M. (1981). *Peabody Picture Vocabulary Test–Revised.* Circle Pines, MN: American Guidance Service.

Ekstein, R., & Wallerstein, R. W. (1958). *The Teaching and Learning of Psychotherapy.* New York: Basic Books.

Elkind, D. (1970, April 5). Erik Erikson's eight ages of man. *New York Times Magazine,* 126–133.

Erikson, E. (1950). *Childhood and Society.* New York: W. W. Norton.

Faber, A., & Mazlish, E. (1982). *How to Talk so Kids Will Listen, and Listen so Kids Will Talk.* New York: Avon Books.

Farley, G. K., & Zimet, S. G. (Eds.). (1991). *Treatment for Children with Emotional Disorders.* Vol. 2, *Models across the Country.* New York: Plenum Press.

Federal Register. (1986, October 8). *Amendments to the Education for All Handicapped Children's Act (PL. 99-457)*.

Fraiberg, S. (1987). *Selected Writings of Selma Fraiberg*. Columbus, OH: State University Press.

Fraiberg, S., Adelson, E., & Shapiro, V. (1975). Ghosts in the nursery: A psychoanalytic approach to the problems of impaired infant-mother relationships. *Journal of Child Psychiatry, 14*(3): 387–422.

French, A. P. (1977). Background of the problem. In *Disturbed Children and Their Families* (98–117). New York: Human Sciences Press.

Freston, C. (1992). *Elementary At-Risk Programs*. Ogden, UT: Ogden School District.

Freud, A. (1954). *Safeguarding the Emotional Health of Our Children*. New York: Child Welfare League.

Freud, A. (1946). *The Ego and the Mechanisms of Defense*. New York: International University Press.

Galambos, J. W. (1969). *Head Start to Confidence*. Washington, DC: Office of Child Development, U. S. Department of Health, Education, Welfare.

Gardner, R. (1979). Helping children cooperate in therapy. In J. Noshpitz (Ed.), *Basic Handbook of Child Psychiatry,* Vol. 3 (414–433). New York: Basic Books.

Ginott, H. G. (1976). Therapeutic intervention in child treatment. In C. E. Schaefer (Ed.), *Therapeutic Use of Child's Play* (279–290). New York: Jason Aaronson.

Goleman, D. (1992, October 4). Psychotherapy and your child. *New York Times Magazine,* 12.

Greenspan, S. I. (1992). Reconsidering the diagnosis and treatment of very young children with autistic spectrum of pervasive developmental disorder. *Zero to Three, 13*(21): 1–9.

Haworth, M. R. (1964). *Child Psychotherapy*. New York: Basic Books.

Helmer, L. and Laliberte, M. (1987). Assessment groups for preschool children: A preventive program. *Archives of Psychiatric Nursing, 1*(5): 27–30.

Hooks, M. Y., Mayes, L. C., & Volkmar, F. R. (1988). Psychiatric disorders among preschool children. *Journal of American Academy of Child and Adolescent Psychiatry, 27*(5): 623–627.

Hutchins, V. L., & McPherson, M. (1991, February). National agenda for children with special health needs. *American Psychologist, 46*(2): 141–143.

Irwin, E. C., & Shapiro, M. (1975). Puppetry as a diagnostic and therapeutic technique. *Psychiatry and Art, 4:* 86–94.

Johnson, M. (1988). Use of play group therapy in promoting social skills. *Issues in Mental Health Nursing, 9*(1): 105–112.

Kagan, J., & Snidman, N. (1991). Temperamental factors in human development. *American Psychologist, 46*(8): 856–862.

Kalmanson, B., & Seligman, S. (1992). Family-provider relationship: The basis of all interventions. *Young Children, 4*(4): 46–52.

Kalmanson, B. (1989). Developmental vulnerabilities. *Early Childhood Update, 5*(4): 5–7.

Knoff, H. M. (1992). Assessment of social emotional functioning and adaptive behavior. In E. V. Nuttal, I. Romero, and J. Kalesnik (Eds.), *Assessing and Screening Preschoolers* (121–143). Boston: Allyn & Bacon.

Koppitz, E. M. (1968). *Psychological Evaluation of Children's Human Figure Drawings.* New York: Grune & Stratton.

Koppitz, E. M. (1975). *The Bender Gestalt Test for Young Children,* Vol. 2. New York: Grune & Stratton.

Krueger, M. S., Fox, R. G., Friedman, J., & Sampson, J. (1987). The generic team approach. *Child and Youth Care Quarterly, 16*(2): 131–144.

Kukic, S. V., & Reavis, H. K. (1991). *Utah Handbook for the Assessment and Clarification of Students Who Are Suspected of Being Behavior Disordered.* Salt Lake City: Utah State Office of Education.

Kukic, S. J. (1988). Master plan for services for students at risk. From *Prevention through Remediation.* Salt Lake City: Utah State Office of Education.

Landy, S., & Peters, R. (1991). Understanding and treating the hyperaggressive toddler. *Zero to Three, 11*(3): 22–31.

Leiter, R. G. (1966). *Leiter International Performance Scale–Arthur Adaptation.* Chicago: Stoelting.

Mahler, M. (1972). On the first three subphases of the separation-individuation process. *International Journal of Psychoanalysis, 53*(3): 333–338.

Martin, R. P. (1988). *The Temperament Assessment Battery for Children (TABC).* Vermont: Clinical Psychology Publishing Company.

Marzollo, J., & Lloyd, J. (1972). *Learning through Play.* New York: Harper.

McCracken, M. (1973). *A Circle of Children.* New York: Harper & Row.

Meisels, S. J., & Shonkoff, J. P. (1989). *Early Intervention: Handbook of Theory, Practice, and Analysis.* New York: Cambridge University Press.

Merrill-Palmer Scale of Mental Tests. (1931). Chicago: Stoelting.

Miller, A. (1981). *The Drama of the Gifted Child.* New York: Basic Books.

Mills, B. (1990, March). The therapeutic use of sand and water play with maternally deprived preschool children. *Association for Play Therapy Newsletter,* No. 9.

Minuchin, S., Montalvo, B., Guerney, B., Rosman, B., & Schuma, F. (1967). *Families of the Slums.* New York: Basic Books.

Mitchell-Meadows, M. (1992, December). Report urges policy makers to focus on childhood issues. *APA Monitor,* 47. Washington, DC.

Morse, W. (1992, Winter). Mental health professionals and teachers: How do the twain meet? *Beyond Behavior, 3*(2): 12–20.

Moustakas, C. E. (1992). *Psychotherapy with Children: The Living Relationship.* Greeley, CO: Carron Publisher.

Murphy, L. B. (1963). *Problems in Recognizing Emotional Disturbance in Children.* New York: Child Welfare League of America.

Newman, R. (1991). Consultations: Redl's influence. *Residential Treatment for Children and Youth, 8*(4): 83–92.

Nuttall, E. V., Romero, I., & Kalesnik, J. (1992). *Assessing and Screening Preschoolers: Psychological and Educational Dimensions.* Boston: Allyn & Bacon.

Ostrom, N. N. (1982). *Some Observations Regarding Group Psychotherapy with Children.* Unpublished paper.

Phares, V. (1992). Where is Poppa? The relative lack of attention to the role of fathers in child and adolescent psychotherapy. *American Psychologist, 47*(5): 657–664.

Phillips, D. A. (1987). *Quality in Child Care: What Does Research Tell Us?* Washington, DC: National Association for the Education of Young Children.

Piaget, J. (1983). Piaget's theory. In P. H. Mussen (Ed.), *Handbook of Child Psychology.* Vol. 1, *History, Theory and Methods* (4th ed.), 703–732. New York: Wiley.

Pine, F. (1985). *Developmental Theory and Clinical Process.* New Haven, CT: Yale University Press.

Play Therapy Bibliography. (1990). Denton, TX: University of North Texas, Center for Play Therapy.

Plenk, A. M. (1978). Activity group therapy for emotionally disturbed preschool children. *Behavior Disorders: Journal of the Council for Children with Behavioral Disorders, 3*(3): 210–218. Also in C. Schaefer, L. Johnson, and J. Wherry (Eds.). (1982). *Group Therapies for Children and Youth* (49). San Francisco: Jossey-Bass. 91–92.

Plenk, A. M. (1986). *Hold Fast to Dreams: A History of The Children's Center and Its Role in the Salt Lake Community, 1962–1986.* Salt Lake City, UT: The Children's Center.

Plenk, A. M., Hinchey, F. S., & Davies, M. U. (1985). *Plenk Storytelling Test.* Salt Lake City, UT: The Children's Center.

Plenk, A. M., & Hinchey, F. S. (1985, March/April). Clinical assessment of maladjusted preschool children. *Child Welfare, 64*(2): 127–134. Washington, DC: Child Welfare League of America.

Powers, D. (1980). *Creating environments for troubled children.* Chapel Hill: University of North Carolina Press.

Redl, F. (1966). *When We Deal with Children.* New York: Free Press.

Redl, F., & Wineman, D. (1957). *The Aggressive Child.* Glencoe, IL: Free Press.

Rose, S., Rose, S., & Feldman, J. (1989). Stability of behavior problems in very young children. *Developmental Psychopathology, 1*(1): 5–19.

Sandler, J., Kennedy, H., & Tyson, R. L. (1980). *The Technique of Child Psychoanalysis: Discussions with Anna Freud.* Cambridge, Mass: Harvard University Press.

Satir, V. (1972). *People Making.* Palo Alto, CA: Science and Behavior Books.

Sattler, J. M. (1988). *Assessment of Children* (3rd ed.). San Diego, CA: Author.

Sayers, J. (1991). *Mothers of psychoanalysis.* New York: W. W. Norton.

Schaefer, C. E. (1976). *Therapeutic Use of Child's Play.* New York: Jason Aaronson.

Schnell, R. R., & Workman-Daniels, K. (1992). Intellectual assessment of preschoolers. In E. V. Nuttal, I. Romero, and J. Kalesnik (Eds.), *Assessing and Screening Preschoolers* (145–192). Boston: Allyn & Bacon.

Schorr, L. B. (1989). *Within Our Reach: Breaking the Cycle of Disadvantage.* New York: Doubleday.

Seligman, S. (1989). Emotional and social development in infancy and early childhood. *Early Childhood Update, 5*(4): 1–2.

Seligman, S., & Pawl, J. (1985). Impediments in the formation of a working alliance in infant-parent psychotherapy. In J. D. Call, E. Galenson, and R. Tyson (Eds.), *Frontiers of Infant Psychiatry,* Vol. 2. New York: Basic Books.

Skinner, B. F. (1974). *About Behaviorism.* New York: Knopf.

Slavson, S. R. (1943). *Introduction to Group Therapy.* New York: Commonwealth Fund.

Slavson, S. R. (1976). Play group therapy. In C. E. Schaefer, *Therapeutic Use of Child's Play* (241–252). New York: Jason Aaronson.

Smith-Taylor, M. (1991, Fall). Volunteers: A valuable tradition at The Children's Center. *Inside.* Salt Lake City, UT: The Children's Center.

Solnit, A. J., Nordhaus, B. F., & Lord, R. (1992). *When Home Is No Haven.* New Haven, CT: Yale University Press.

Solnit, A. J. (1990, December). The Bowlby legacy: Continuity in theory building. *Readings, 5*(4): 4–7.

Sutton-Smith, B. (1985, October). The child at play. *Psychology Today,* 64–65.

Terman, L. M., & Merrill, M. A. (1973). *Stanford Binet Intelligence Scale: Form L-M* (1972 norms ed.). Boston: Houghton Mifflin.

Thomas, A., & Chess, S. (1977). *Temperament and Development.* New York: Brunner/Mazel.

Thorndike, R. L., Hager, E. P., & Sattler, J. M. (1986). *Guide for Administering and Scoring the Stanford-Binet Intelligence Scale* (4th ed.). Chicago: Riverside Publ.

Tyler, A., & Gregory, V. R. (1992). Assessment of physical and sexual abuse in the preschool child. In E. V. Nuttal, I. Romero, and J. Kalesnik (Eds.), *Assessing and Screening Preschoolers* (369–382). Boston: Allyn & Bacon.

Vinter, R. (1974). Program Activities: An analysis of their effects on participant behavior. In M. Sundel, P. Glasser, R. Sarri, R. Vinter (eds.) *Individual Change Through Small Groups* (233–243). New York. Free Press.

Walker, C. (1988). Use of art and play therapy in pediatric oncology. *Journal of the Association of Pediatric Oncology, Nurses, 5*(1–2): 34.

Webb, N. (1991). *Play Therapy with Children in Crisis: A Casebook for Practitioners.* New York: Guilford Press.

Whittaker, J. K. (1974). Program activities: Their selection and use in a therapeutic milieu. In P. Glasser, R. Sarri, and R. Vinter (Eds.), *Individual Change through Small Groups.* New York: Free Press. *The Other 23 Hours: Child Care Work with Emotionally Disturbed Children in a Therapeutic Milieu.* New York: Aldine de Gruyter.

Whittaker, J. K., & Small, R. W. (1977). Differential approaches to group treatment of children and adolescents. *Child & Youth Services, 1*(1): 5–15.

Whittaker, J. K. (Ed.). (1979). *Caring for Troubled Children: Residential Treatment in a Community Context.* San Francisco: Jossey-Bass.

Wood, M. (Ed.). (1975). *Developmental therapy.* Baltimore: University Park Press.

Young, T., Dore, M., & Pappenfort, D. (1989). Trends in residential group care: 1966–1982. In E. A. Balcerzak (Ed.), *Group Care of Children: Transitions toward the Year 2000* (11–35). Washington, DC: Child Welfare League of America.

Zilbach, J. J. (1986). *Young Children in Family Therapy.* New York: Brunner/Mazel.

Zimet, S. G., & Farley, G. K. (Eds.). (1991). *Day Treatment for Children with Emotional Disorders.* Vol. 1, *A Model in Action.* New York: Plenum Press.

Zwerdling, E. (1974). *The ABC of Case Work with Children.* New York: Child Welfare League.

Index

About the Author

AGNES M. PLENK was founder and executive director of The Children's Center in Salt Lake City and now serves the center as psychology consultant. She is the originator of the Plenk Storytelling Test (PST), a projective test for young children. She is Adjunct Professor in Clinical Psychology and Educational Psychology at the University of Utah and Brigham Young University.